Narco-Terrorism

A Unified Strategy
to Fight a Growing Terrorist Menace

Douglas J. Davids

Transnational Publishers, Inc.

Published and distributed by Transnational Publishers, Inc.
410 Saw Mill River Road
Ardsley, NY 10502, USA

Phone: 914-693-5100
Fax: 914-693-4430
E-mail: info@transnationalpubs.com
Web: www.transnationalpubs.com

Library of Congress Cataloging-in-Publication Data

Davids, Dougals J., 1964–
    Narco-terrorism : a unified strategy to fight a growing terrorist menace / Dougals
J. Davids.
    p.cm.
    Includes bibliographical references.
    ISBN 1–57105–249–6
    1. Drug traffic—Political aspects. 2. Terrorism—Economic aspects. 3. Narcot-
ics, Control of. 4. Terrorism—Prevention. I. Title

HV5801 .D27 2002
363.45—dc21   2002018000

Manufactured in the United States of America

Dedicated to my mom and dad,
who gave me every hope and chance.

*The victorious strategist seeks battle
after the victory has been won,
while he who is destined to defeat
first fights and seeks victory afterwards.*
Sun Tzu

*I don't underrate the value of military knowledge,
but if men make war in slavish observance to rules,
they will fail.*
U.S. Grant

DISCLAIMER:

The strategy presented in this book is strictly the opinion of the author, and is intended only for academic discussion and thought. It is not known nor intended to reflect the policies of the Department of Defense, or any national office, agency, or organization.

Contents

Foreword

The initial idea for this book began in 1990 when I told a friend, who was a casual user of illegal drugs, that her drug "hobby" financed terrorism. After hearing a brief explanation of what I meant, she quit using drugs almost immediately—and permanently. I realized from this single event that education about narco-terrorism could be a potent tool in stopping illegal drug use. Over the next few years, as I studied the link between drug trafficking and terrorism, identifying its strengths and weaknesses, I further discussed my narco-terrorism education ideas with late teens and young adults. By 1995 I had developed a four-phased conceptual strategy to defeat narco-terrorism with education about narco-terrorism as the key.

In 1997, I began graduate studies at Louisiana State University (LSU) and my narco-terrorism research became my thesis. LSU afforded me two superb opportunities. First, I was able to work with a highly respected international law professor, Dr. Christopher Blakesley, who provided essential guidance in researching the legal aspects of the matters discussed in this book. Second, the Department of Psychology provided resources and assistance to me in developing and conducting an exploratory survey to prove that educating teens and young adults on narco-terrorism could significantly decrease drug demand in this country. Coincidently, in December 2001, the Partnership for a Drug Free America conducted a simple three-question survey among teens and young adults to see if education about narco-terrorism would be a good anti-drug education tool. Their results are clearly in line with mine. I have since shared some of my information on narco-terrorism education with them.

By 1998 the specific strategic plan described in this book was complete, although I made some updates to the manuscript to complete my thesis requirement in 2000. Shortly thereafter my peers suggested that I seek publication of my strategy, but I delayed. I didn't want to give the "enemy" the chance to read the plan before it possibly could be put into action. Earlier, I had engaged in something the military calls "wargaming." That is, I undertook a role reversal exercise and accepted the persona of the enemy to try to determine how my plan could be defeated.

First, I decided there would be three "enemies." One enemy would be the terrorists and insurgents themselves, who would not want the "image" of their "revolution" tainted with drug trafficking, let alone lose their biggest means of financial support. Nor would the drug traffickers (my second enemy) want their market to know that the money spent to buy the drugs went to terrorist organizations. A third potential enemy to the strategy would be the drug legalists. In this case my fear was that, in further support of their claim that the drug war can never be won, they would use my narco-terrorism information as another pretext for legalizing drugs.

My idea in executing this strategy was to use two of the most important principles of war — *surprise* and *offense*. I would use documentaries, television, radio, billboards, and every other imaginable means of public communication to saturate, overnight if possible, the country with a wake-up call on narco-terrorism *and* the problems of drug legalization. This education program would be launched with such speed and intensity that the narco-terrorists and drug legalists would be suddenly put on the defensive. The value of getting this head start with a well-executed education program had been reinforced by my study of the Communist propaganda campaigns which were so successfully conducted around the world during the Cold War. Information and disinformation campaigns were common on both sides during the Cold War, and in this strategy—a perfectly legitimate one used throughout history—the Communists had been very successful. However, my strategy would have a major advantage over most such campaigns in that my narco-terrorism education would tell the truth. Disinformation is common in foreign countries with which one is at war (even "Cold" war), but a government must always tell the truth to its own people lest it lose credibility.

So one might ask why publish this now? The reason is that since 11 September the link between drug trafficking and terrorism has gained increasing media attention, and the possible application of a "surprise offensive" is no longer feasible. So now, the purpose of publishing this book must be to shed a new light on a dark, unfamiliar issue. Before the 9/11 attacks, this plan was a "stand alone" strategy; that is, the battle against narco-terrorism would be a fought in its own arena with little outside influence. But since 9/11, this strategy must coincide with both the current *and future* policies of the War on Terrorism, and only a few people in this country can make that decision.

The greatest difficulty in publishing this book came in trying to take a manuscript that was several years old (the majority of which was written before the Colombia Plan), update it, edit it, and publish it as quickly as possible. I'm certain there are experts who could criticize some of the data of the first few chapters, which have become dated in the rapidly changing worlds of drug trafficking and terrorism. But the intent of those early chapters is to describe the *environment* of narco-terrorism—something that has *not* changed. Chapter 4, which discusses the strategy to fight the problem of narco-terrorism, is the key chapter in this book. Unfortunately, my strategy is not entirely complete, as I had intended to do more research on Latin American economics and trade, as well as write a chapter on the problems with drug legalization. It is hoped that this work will spur added impetus to continue more in-depth study in these areas.

I can hardly say that the publication of this strategy is the end of the effort. If accepted, it still needs to be implemented, and in the words of retired Army General Dennis Reimer, "guidance and briefings alone will not guarantee good execution." This strategy must be executed properly, only then can this country and the world make the difficult, but critical, transfer from words to actions.

Douglas J. Davids

December 1, 2001

Introduction

Over the past century the problem of illegal drug flow and abuse throughout the Western Hemisphere has increased steadily. For more than thirty-five years the sales of illegal narcotics have helped support terrorism and military insurgencies[1] throughout the world.[2] The financial profits from illegal drugs have enabled terrorists and guerrilla forces to purchase the arms, munitions, and other military equipment and supplies necessary to carry out insurgencies and terrorist operations. This "narco" relationship with such organizations eventually became known as "narco-terrorism."

With the fall of the Soviet Union—a major source of direct and indirect supplies for many of the world's terrorist and insurgent organizations—terrorist-insurgent narcotics involvement increased, as many of these organizations sought a new means of support. Terrorists who became involved in the drug trade accumulated large sums of money in a short time, and with these funds came the ability to buy armaments, attract new followers, and develop political influence.[3]

Now, in the wake of the "9/11" terrorist attack, and the media attention to the Taliban's financial support from heroin and opium trafficking, America is getting a quick, although limited, education in narco-terrorism. In past years, however, the United States had not wholly accepted the concept of a narcotics-terrorism (or insurgent) relationship—something the Latin American community, for instance, takes for granted. "One does not know if the drug trafficker is a guerrilla or if the guerrilla is a drug trafficker," the director of the Colombian national police declared in 1997. "The line is now blurred; it is a brotherhood community."[4]

But in the United States some officials have tended to regard "narco-terrorism" as a political slogan that was "in line with a familiar vision of the United States besieged by foreign devils."[5] Perhaps the *Washington Times* encapsulated the situation when it stated "U.S. Ambassador to Colombia Myles Frechette, underscoring what many officials in Washington *want* to ignore [italics added], declared that most Colombian rebels are involved in drug smuggling."[6] In the early 1990s the word "narco-terrorism" was taboo within an American embassy of a leading coca-producing country, and a major United States government agency completely denied the existence of the phenomenon. Only recently has the linkage begun to receive any acceptance from the United States government. The former director of the Office of National Drug Control Policy, General (Retired) Barry McCaffrey, is among the convinced, and the Department of Defense has even adopted an official definition of narco-terrorism, which I will review later.

It is possible that the U.S.'s previous unwillingness to accept the concept of narco-terrorism may be based on a belief that such acknowledgement would mean a much steeper escalation in the drug war. That is, if the U.S. were willing to admit officially that terrorist-insurgent groups are involved in narco-trafficking, then the U.S. would feel obligated to fight these forces with an equally capable force—the military—in order to achieve victory in the drug war. It is no secret that the U.S. is fond of neither insurgent nor guerrilla wars (such as the Vietnam War).

Nonetheless, the use of conventional military forces is a typical U.S. response to such a problem. When the U.S. sees a formidable enemy with effective and plentiful munitions, it often uses its world-dominant military to execute forceful courses of action, such as bombing raids (Kosovo), or occupation duty (Somalia, Haiti). A noted expert of Colombian guerrilla warfare, Alfredo Molano, whose war-torn country is attempting peace negotiations with the successful and heavily narco-financed Colombian guerrillas, even commented that if "the U.S. ever accepts the narco-guerrilla thesis, it's the end of the peace negotiations."[7] Yet such a response in a guerrilla conflict is as direct an approach as a frontal assault on an enemy army in a well-established, defensive position. This author, in contrast to such a direct approach, advocates a four-phased strategy for fighting narco-terrorism using the *indirect approach* (as termed by military theorist B.H. Liddell Hart).

The first chapter of this book provides a legal definition of narco-terrorism, and discusses the relationship between narco-traffickers and terrorist-insurgent organizations. Chapter 2 provides an overview of narco-terrorism worldwide, covering such regions as Latin America, Southwest Asia, and Southeast Asia. Chapter 3 explains how the nations of the Western Hemisphere have attempted to combat drugs and terrorism/insurgencies as separate issues, and why this policy has been such a failure. The fourth chapter demonstrates how knowledge of narco-terrorism can be used to fight both problems successfully, using Latin America as the primary proving. It demonstrates how four currently independent efforts—Education, Extradition, a Specialized Force, and Civic Action—can support one another effectively in implementing what I call the *"Unified Strategy."* Drug addiction treatment, though an important part of the drug problem which should not be underestimated, is fully supported by this author; however, because it is not in itself an element of this strategy, I do not discuss it here.

In this book I focus primarily on Latin American narco-terrorism because most illegal drugs used in the U.S.—but not produced within this country—come from Latin America. From Colombia we get cocaine, heroin, and marijuana, while from Mexico we obtain two types of heroin (Black Tar and Brown Powder heroin), marijuana, and methamphetamines (a drug which Mexican drug cartels still seems to control the US market), as well as more cocaine that originated in Colombia. Jamaica also provides a moderate amount of marijuana to the United States. The only internationally produced drug we receive in mass quantity from countries outside of Latin America is the drug commonly called "Ecstasy," which originally derived from Europe, and is heavily controlled by the Russian and Israeli Mafias. However, Colombian and Mexican traffickers are quickly gaining control of the U.S. market for this lucrative product. Ecstasy production is also emerging in the United States, Canada, and China. The U.S. also receives moderate amounts of marijuana from Canada (known as "BC Bud"), some heroin and methamphetamines from Southeast Asia, and a very small amount of heroin from Southwest Asia. Illegal drugs produced domestically include marijuana, methamphetamines, synthetic drugs such as LSD, and some prescription drugs which are increasingly being abused.

While parts of this book focus solely on fighting the war on drugs, we must understand that in doing so we are actually accomplishing a twofold purpose: curtailing the supply of drugs from international sources in the United States, which in turns prevents the return of drug revenues to terrorist and insurgent organizations. This is not to say that stopping the drug supply from terrorist organizations will wipe out all their funding, as most such groups have other means of support. Nor is this strategy intended to completely eliminate the drug problem in America, as many illegal drugs used in the United States are not associated with terrorist organizations, such as the increasing abuse of prescription drugs. However, what this strategy can do is restrict American consumption of illegal drugs from international sources, thereby stopping a significant base of funding for terrorist organizations. This, in turn, permits all the large amounts of funding, resources, and assets used to interdict illegal drugs at our borders to go to domestic counterdrug efforts such as federal, state, and local law enforcement agencies, anti-drug community based organizations, addiction treatment efforts, as well as general education and human development programs for youths.

We begin by defining and explaining an often misunderstood and loosely used term—narco-terrorism.

Chapter I

Narco-Terrorism Defined and Explained

The relationship between terrorist-insurgent groups and narco-trafficking is commonly referred to as "narco-terrorism" or "narco-insurgency." But are these fair labels? Ronald Reagan stated that "one man's terrorist is another man's freedom fighter." Is a terrorist really just a freedom fighter, and is terrorism just another form of warfare for the powerless? Should the term "narco-terrorism" be changed to a more impartial term? Are acts of violence by insurgent forces against innocent people acts of terrorism or merely war crimes, and what is the difference? This chapter answers these questions by defining both terrorism and narco-terrorism in contrast with war crimes and narco-insurgency, respectively. It also describes how the illegal drug trade significantly finances narco-terrorism.

Louis Rene Beres, Professor of International Law in the Department of Political Science at Purdue University, has argued that the "failure [of insurgents] to comply with such restrictions [the laws of war] does not convert these military forces into terrorists, but it does make them guilty of war crimes and possibly even crimes against humanity."[1] To a degree Beres is correct, but some clarification of what constitutes an act of terrorism, as opposed to acts of war and acts against the laws of war, is necessary.

The U.S. Department of Defense (DoD) defines terrorism as "the calculated use of violence or threat of violence to instill fear, intended to coerce or try to intimidate governments or societies in the pursuit of goals that are political, religious, or ideological."[2] Unfortunately, at this time there is no fully accepted international definition of terrorism. Some scholars, however, provide definitions of terrorism that go a long way toward resolving the thorny issues that surround this phenomenon.

Christopher Blakesley, Professor of International Law at Louisiana State University, has defined terrorism as

> . . . the application of terror-violence against innocent individuals for the purpose of obtaining thereby some military, political, or philosophical end from a third-party government or group. The third-party government or group may be another government, one's own government, one's own people, or another people which the perpetrators are attempting to intimidate, influence, overthrow, or oppress.[3]

According to Blakesley, terrorism consists of five elements:[4]

1) the perpetration of violence by whatever means;
2) the targeting of innocents;
3) the intent to cause violence with wanton disregard for its consequences;
4) the purpose of coercing or intimidating an enemy or otherwise to obtain some political, military, or religious benefit; and
5) conducting the above acts without justification or excuse.

Essentially, Blakesley implies that terrorism is violence aimed at innocents (or non-combatants) to gain an edge over, or to coerce, a third party. This differs from justifiable and legal revolutionary violence, which seeks liberation from oppression or restriction on one's own sovereignty (assuming such acts of revolutionary violence fall within the law of war).[5]

For example, the attack of Colombian M-19 guerrillas on the Colombian Palace of Justice in 1985 where they killed noncombatants and civilians with the intent to coerce a third party to stop extradition of drug lords to the United States, or the murder of babies by Peruvian guerrillas to coerce the local people to follow Shining Path rule, were blatant acts of terrorism under Blakesley's definition.

Another definition describes terrorism as an act designed to "induce a state of fear in the victim" [a non-combatant], which is "ruthless and does not conform to humanitarian norms, and that [uses] publicity [as] an essential factor in terrorist strategy."[6] This definition dissects terrorism a little more deeply and provides additional guidance in distinguishing between terrorism and war. It shows that publicity is a key factor in distinguishing acts of terrorism from acts contrary to the laws of war, "for the purpose of coercing or intimidating an enemy (government or group) or otherwise to obtain some political, military, or religious benefit."[7] During the My Lai massacre, the American platoon leader on the ground was not trying to intimidate or coerce anyone, and he certainly did not want the publicity he received for his actions. That incident is considered a war crime. However, when German soldiers on the eastern front during World War II executed innocent civilians one by one for each German soldier killed, the intent was to intimidate or coerce the Soviets into losing their will to fight. Such an act is terrorism. Even though not all terrorist groups desire international publicity for violent acts-as do many Muslim extremists in seeking world attention to their cause-publicity (local or national) is normally required to achieve control through intimidation.

Taking into account the above definitions of terrorism (using key terms such as "violence against non-combatants," "coercion," and "publicity"), what constitutes narco-terrorism? Could it be terrorism by senior drug traffickers for the purpose of enhancing their trafficking operations, or possibly terrorism by insurgents who are linked (for financial revenues) to the international drug trade?

In reference to drug traffickers who use terrorism to assist their drug trafficking operations, some argue that "narco-terrorism" is a flawed term because narcotics traffickers-even when committing violent acts-do not have an ideology for which they are fighting. Therefore, it is claimed, they are nothing more than violent thugs, as opposed to bona fide terrorists who are fighting for a cause. Yet while drug lords may in fact be "violent thugs," they, like insurgents, also have goals and ideologies-they merely want to achieve different ends. Drug lords are capitalists who want to expand their wealth and status, while most insurgents (particularly Latin American-based insurgents) generally want to destroy the incumbent capitalist (or capitalist-backed) government.[8] And even though various insurgent groups and drug lords may have different goals, their methods are often the same-terrorism (as defined above). Insurgent-terrorists are simply insurgents attempting to overthrow a government using terrorism as one method. Drug lords, on the other hand, are not attempting to overthrow any government. Rather, their aim is to use terrorism to disrupt a government's ability to stop the drug flow. As Andrew Campbell puts it:

> These drug cartels are more like terrorist organizations than a group of disunified (sic) outlaws. They have an identifiable political aim to "neutralize the state."[9] Yet unlike the Palestinian Liberation Organization-which seeks the establishment of an independent state-or the Irish Republican Army-which seeks the independence of Northern Ireland...it [the Medellín cartel] merely seeks "to thwart reaction by the healthy

part of society"[10] in order to advance its own criminal activity.[11]

The Colombian drug lords-who today are made up of smaller splinter groups of the major cartels of the 1980s and early 1990s-have made it clear that they seek: (1) to coerce certain governmental officials into certain acts, such as preventing extradition to the United States (exemplified during the M-19 attack on the Palace of Justice); and (2) to neutralize a State in which illegal drugs are being trafficked (whether in Colombia or other trans-shipment countries) in order to keep that area's flow of drugs free from interference. Neither Blakesley nor the other authors state or imply that acts of terrorism need be only political or subversive in nature, but must simply "coerce a third party." Drug lords primarily want to make money, but they often employ terrorist acts to accomplish that goal.

The U.S. Department of Defense (DoD) agrees. It defines narco-terrorism as follows:

> Terrorism [is] conducted to further the aims of drug traffickers. It may include assassinations, extortion, hijackings, bombings, and kidnappings directed against judges, prosecutors, elected officials, or law enforcement agents, and general disruption of a legitimate government to divert attention from drug operations.[12]

But what about the relationship between insurgent-terrorist organizations and drug trafficking-that proceeds from drug trafficking operations are a viable source of funding for insurgent-terrorist operations (to coerce governments and peoples) which otherwise could not be conducted without these revenues? This linkage requires proof of a symbiotic relationship between the two. As stated in the introduction, the existence of this relationship has been denied over much of the past decade for various reasons, and only now is the nation as a whole beginning to understand this correlation.

The means by which financial revenues from drug trafficking finance insurgent-terrorist organizations are explained and described in the second chapter. It is probably safe to say that most people in the counterdrug business understand that insurgent-terrorist groups, such as those that operate in Colombia, use the revenues from drug trafficking to finance their organization. Therefore, this author submits a two-fold definition of narco-terrorism. On the one hand (and in relation to the DoD definition) is terrorism that aims to protect and support the activities of illegal drug traffickers; and on the other, terrorism by organizations that use the financial profits of narco-trafficking to support their political, religious, or other goals. The latter part of the definition can include insurgent organizations that use terrorism as a method.

The possible weakness in this narco-terrorism definition can be summarized in the earlier quoted statement that "one man's terrorist is another man's freedom fighter," or insurgent. Terrorism is often warfare for the weak. That is, persecuted people attempting to gain freedom may have little choice but to use violence and intimidation to achieve their goals, and they may use narco-trafficking to support such warfare. Some people may see acts of terrorism as desperate measures to support personal freedom. They might even have a population's support to conduct such acts. However, one cannot legally, or morally, justify the death of an innocent bystander or otherwise uninvolved person for any cause.

The difference between narco-terrorism and narco-insurgency is that narco-terrorists use terrorism (as defined above) as a tactic or method of operating, whether they are drug traffickers or insurgents. On the other hand, narco-insurgents are those who use the financial profits of narco-trafficking to support their goals of subversion, but do not use terrorism as a tactic to achieve such goals. Perhaps, in this case, one would prefer to further define narco-terrorism as "Drug Financed Terrorism" (DFT), and narco-insurgency as "Drug Financed Warfare" (DFW).

With the above explanations of "narco-terrorism" and "terrorism", it is now possible to discuss how narco-terrorism operates by describing the production and smuggling of illegal drugs, and the symbiotic relationship between terrorist-insurgent organizations and drug trafficking, using Latin America as an example. However, as we shall see in the next chapter, we could just as well be describing opium and heroin smuggling operations in Southwest Asia-trafficked to Russia and Europe-which are heavily controlled by Islamic extremists such as the Taliban and the Kosovo Liberation Army (as well as Turkish, Russian, Albanian, and Nigerian smugglers), or similar operations in Southeast Asia, were opiates are produced within the "Golden Triangle" by groups such as the Wa'a State in Myanmar, and trafficked by Chinese crime syndicates throughout Eastern Asia and North America. In focusing on Latin America, my intent is simply to exemplify how drugs are trafficked from the production country to their final destination, and to elucidate the part most terrorist/insurgent organizations play in this role.

Coca (for cocaine), marijuana, and opiates (for heroin) grow in various Latin American countries (such as Colombia or Peru), often under the protective umbrella of terrorist and/or insurgent organizations that protect, and sometimes control, the processing of the substances through cultivation, production, and initial transportation. Once converted into an illegal drug, the product is transported, for sale and consumption, primarily to the United States and Europe.

Trafficking to the U.S. in the 1970s and early 1980s went primarily through the Caribbean Sea to Florida, with Miami as the hub. (Such well-known smuggling operations gave birth to television shows such as "Miami Vice.") However, as U.S. interdiction efforts concentrated on the Caribbean smuggling routes, traffickers began to move operations to Mexico-a country which has a history as a "smuggling platform."[13] All types of smuggling operations-alcohol, migrant workers, weapons, automobiles, electronics, and others-has been occurring between the U.S. and Mexico for decades. Then came the North American Free Trade Agreement (NAFTA). It has often been said that what NAFTA did for trade, it also did for drug trafficking. Smugglers on the Mexican-American border were already well organized, and the long Mexican-U.S. border created enormous difficulties for the U.S. and Mexican patrols endeavoring to stop them.[14] Prior to NAFTA, smugglers operated over the desert, in the air, or through complex tunnel systems. Now, however, under the auspices of NAFTA, they can slip past customs agents in the immense amount of legal traffic that passes through the border on a daily basis.

To add to the interdiction problem, corruption within Mexico is notorious. Only a couple years ago, Andres Oppenheimer, Pulitzer Prize co-winner and senior Latin American correspondent for the Miami Herald, described in his book, *Bordering on Chaos,* how corruption and deceit are accepted practice in modern-day Mexico. He goes so far as to say that the word "truth" has a negative connotation, citing the example of Coca-Cola's slogan "It's the real thing." When translated into Spanish (*Esta es la verdad*) it means, "This is the truth," an assertion that allegedly was received negatively by the Mexican people.[15] Corruption (which drug traffickers thrive on), combined with millions of dollars in drug money, has greatly hindered efforts of honest authorities to defeat drug smuggling in Mexico. While the former and current presidents of Mexico, Ernesto Zedillo and Vicente Fox, respectively, both made great strides in ending the corruption, the problem is still overwhelming.

Mexico is still the most important point of entry for drugs reaching the United States. In recent years, however, smugglers have turned increasingly back to the Caribbean. The reason, according to Warren Richey, staff writer of the Christian Science Monitor, is that the Colombian drug lords are "plagued by increasingly greedy Mexican middlemen and beefed-up law enforcement on America's Southwest border."[16] Sandor Calvani, chief of the Caribbean office of the United Nations Drug Control Program, adds that the current geographical setting of the Western Hemisphere is "probably the best scenario a drug trafficker could invent. In the south, big producing countries, and up north, big consuming countries. And in between, 1,200 islands organized in 29 countries with four different [government] systems that do not communicate among themselves [with] an infinite number of coves and small beaches."[17] Additionally, bribing officials is easy and comparatively cheap in the poor Caribbean islands. Poverty-stricken Haiti, where bribes are simple and hungry people are willing to do any kind of work, is a favorite transportation site. Haiti's weak government and institutions, the police included, provide no real threat to the traffickers.

Puerto Rico is also a favorite smuggling platform because once drugs are on the island-a U.S. commonwealth-the traffickers are no longer required to go through customs to enter the U.S.[18] In 1999, studies indicated that 57 percent of illegal narcotics went through Mexico, 33 percent through the Caribbean islands, and 12 percent through Central America.[19] However, these numbers fluctuate year by year.

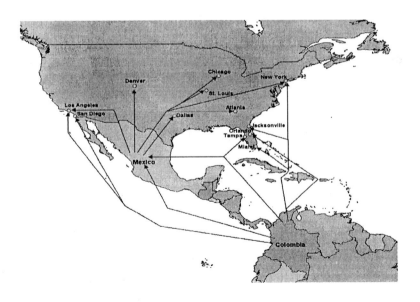

Latin American Drug Flow
Information source: Drug Enforcement Administration
Map made by Digital Mapping Center

The flexibility of the traffickers operating throughout various regions reveals why interdiction methods have not been able to stop the drug flow. The traffickers, in mimicking General Douglas MacArthur's strategic maxim in the South Pacific, simply "go where the enemy ain't." This strategy is as old as warfare itself. Sun Tzu, the ancient military strategist and general, wrote in his famous book, *The Art of War:* "Should [the enemy] strengthen his left, he will weaken his right; should he strengthen his right, he will weaken his left. If he sends reinforcements everywhere, he will be everywhere weak."[20] In other words, one knows where the enemy is weak if he knows where the enemy is strong. Therefore, exploit the enemy's weakness. If interdiction efforts are concentrated in the Caribbean, move to Mexico. If they are concentrated in Mexico, move to the Caribbean. If the U.S. attempts to concentrate in both areas with its current force and budget, it will be weak in both places. If the U.S. doubles the amount of manpower, logistics, and the billions of dollars already dedicated to the interdiction effort and concentrates in both regions, the traffickers can smuggle through the Gulf States, the Pacific, or any part of the expansive U.S.-Canadian border. The New York Times correctly referred to the problem as "the impossibility of choking all the trafficking routes that shift nimbly through South American countries."[21]

Similarly, eradication efforts, that is, efforts to destroy drug-producing plants by any means, are revealing similar problems as interdiction efforts. For example, eradication efforts in Colombia's Guaviare area did reduce coca growing for that region. However, cultivation of coca was moved to guerrilla-controlled areas of Putumayo and Caqueta, where the overall production of coca increased 25 percent in 1998.[22] The drug lords simply move their operations. In 1999, when President Bill Clinton appeared to put greater domestic and international emphasis on the drug war than ever before in his administration, heroin production in Colombia increased 23 percent from the previous year. At the same time satellite photos showed that Colombia produced three times more cocaine than the Central Intelligence Agency had predicted.[23] This is why interdiction and eradication, though necessary, should not be the central focuses of a counter-narcotic strategy. The drug traffickers will simply move "to where the enemy ain't." In Southwest Asia, when Pakistan pressured heroin and opium cultivation out of their country in the mid-1990s, it simply shifted to Afghanistan.

Once the drugs are in the United States they are transported to Los Angeles, Chicago, Miami, New York, and other major cities. From the major cities the drugs are further distributed to smaller buyers (distributors), and then transported to other cities and sold to dealers, and finally to users.

The money from the illegal drug user travels in the reverse direction. Much of this money is transported in bulk cash back out of the United States to Mexico, the Caribbean, or directly to Colombia. It is then laundered through phony businesses, or corrupt financial institutions, and required proceeds are given to major drug traffickers in both the drug-production and drug-transit countries such as Colombia, Mexico, and the Caribbean Islands. Part of the money received by the drug lords in the major producing countries, such as Colombia, pays terrorist and insurgent organizations to continue growing and producing illegal drugs, or to provide security and support for narco-trafficking operations. The terrorists and insurgents use the money to buy military supplies to conduct their terrorist and warfare activities. At other times, the drug lords use their transportation assets to provide arms and weapons to the terrorists and insurgents, instead of paying them cash.

Ironically, some insurgent organizations initially frowned upon drug trafficking for any purposes. The religious views of the Afghanistan's Taliban, for instance, certainly should not have allowed their use of the heroin trade to finance their war (their ban of poppy growth will be discussed in another chapter). Meanwhile, the Colombian Revolutionary Armed Forces of Colombia (or the "FARC," the acronym of their name in Spanish–*Fuerzas Armada Revolucionárias de Colombia*) initially frowned upon the narco-trafficking, and opposed drug use. Originally, the FARC's goals were ideological, and they began working with the narco-traffickers solely to fund their socialist cause. However, the younger generation of FARC insurgents seems to have lower ideological standards and is more interested in personal gain by any means-including drug trafficking and terrorism. Dr. Thomas Hargrove, former eleven-month hostage of the Colombian FARC, seems to agree with this perception.[24] Hargrove, who was working in Colombia with the International Center for Tropical Agriculture to help people in poverty-stricken areas increase food production, was taken hostage by the FARC, who-while claiming to be fighting on behalf of the same constituency-held him for a $6 million ransom. Hargrove also found that his captives, who alleged that they were following the ideals of Ché Guevara, had no clear concept what the ideas of Ché Guevara were really about. Hargrove himself was in fact the one who educated them on the matter.[25]

Hargrove presented an unflattering picture of the FARC guerrillas:

> Some people have an illusion that the FARC guerrillas are idealists, even disenchanted leftists who fight injustices of Colombian society. The people who held me were illiterate and semiliterate children. . . . They

learned their moral values from FARC.

Don't assume that their lack of education reflects the deprivation in which they were raised; few could have gotten past the third grade if they'd been born in the Kennedy family.... One of the most frightening aspects of my captivity, in fact, was the knowledge that I was held by persons who weren't intelligent enough to understand the consequences of their actions.

They claim to follow the principles of Ché Guevara, but they don't even understand Communism. I heard the Comandante say to his troops in formation "Colombia will soon be a revolutionary Communist nation, like Cuba, China, and Japan."

The guerillas use drugs. . . . The most dangerous times for me were when the guerrillas were stoned on a combination of basuco [a by-product of cocaine processing] and brandy, and shooting their weapons randomly. I was almost executed during one such session.[26]

In March 1999 the FARC kidnapped and executed three American foreign aid workers.[27] The Americans were activists working with indigenous Colombian tribes-the same people the FARC claims to be supporting-to stop oil companies from moving onto their land. Yet, regardless of the FARCs ideological incoherence and lack of sophistication, these guerrillas have become an enormous power in Colombia because of the army they have built with hundreds of millions of dollars in drug money.

Coincidentally, Hargrove discovered firsthand the FARC's relationship with drug trafficking, and even informed me (as well as a Congressional House Committee) that the guerrilla camps in which he was held were actually drug laboratories.[28] In his book Long March to Freedom, a diary of his captivity, Hargrove commonly refers to his Colombian captors as "narco-guerrillas" and "illiterate criminals."

To say that terminating terrorists' financing from narco-trafficking would end terrorist activities is, of course, incorrect. These organizations often have secondary and tertiary means of income. The FARC, for example, makes hundreds of millions of dollars from abductions of wealthy Colombian citizens and foreigners, like Hargrove. Colombia has reported 4,925 abductions in the past 3½ years, crediting leftist guerrillas with two-thirds of these kidnappings.[29] Muslim extremists often receive funds from terrorist supporting states such as Iraq, along with more mundane crimes such as credit card theft. However, the financial support received from narco-trafficking is substantial and usually yields great profit. In 1996 the Colombian Military Forces estimated that, of the $1.233 billion appropriated by the guerrillas, $746.6 million of it came from narco-trafficking, $262.2 million from extortion, and $224.4 million from kidnapping.[30] Additionally, narco-trafficking provides a small, still weakly organized insurgency with quick income without attracting the public attention that a kidnapping would.

Narco-terrorism is a real and definable phenomenon. It is a process of illegally financing activities that, in turn, are also illegal. The next chapter examines the origins of narco-terrorism in Latin America-where the problem is perhaps more prevalent than elsewhere in the world-and also provides a brief discussion of narco-terrorism in Southwest and Southeast Asia.

Chapter 2
Narco-Terrorist Relationships

The history of narco-terrorism in Latin America began when Fidel Castro's Cuban regime began using illegal drug sales to finance revolutionary causes throughout Latin America in what could be labeled as narco-insurgency. "Narco" financing of warfare grew when the financially strapped Shining Path, which funded its activities by taxing illegal drug traffickers, conducted a reign of terror throughout Peru in the 1980s and 1990s. Finally, Colombia became a narco-terrorist "Superstate." This section provides an account of the genesis of these developments, and also shows how the problem of narco-terrorism has become a worldwide phenomenon.

Cuba: It Began with Narco-Insurgency

Rachel Ehrenfeld has documented how two Latin American regimes—Fidel Castro's Cuba and the former Sandinista government of Nicaragua—became complicit with the illicit drug trade. It began in Castro's Cuba. "From early on," one author has stated, "it was Castro's policy to aid and abet traffickers in order to subvert American society, finance arms, and bankroll Latin American revolutionaries."[1] Florida Congressman Lincoln Diaz Balart has called Castro "one of the biggest drug traffickers in the world."[2] "There is no question in my mind that Cuba is involved," stated Congressman Dan Burton, co-author of the 1996 law that intensifies the economic embargo on Cuba.[3] Captain Robert B. Workman of the United States Coast Guard and Senior Fellow at the National Defense University during 1984 documented Castro's actions:

> In 1958, Fidel Castro stated publicly that he was going to export his revolution beyond Cuba using "his" methods. His methods included a two-fold purpose for involvement with the narcotics trade: to damage United States society by aiding drug traffickers and to finance Marxist terrorists and guerrilla activity in LATAM [Latin America], including training and arms shipments for insurgency.[4]

Even before Castro won his revolution in Cuba, he believed that his true war would be with the democratic superpower to the north. In a letter to a friend, Castro wrote: "When this war is over, a much longer and more important war will begin for me: [that] I shall have to wage against the Americans. I feel this is my destiny."[5] Unable to fight the United States directly, he apparently chose drugs as one method to damage American society and to finance communist insurgencies in Latin America. After the Cuban revolution, several thousand Cuban drug dealers coincidentally set up operations in the United States, mostly in Miami. In 1966, at the "First Conference of Solidarity of the Peoples of Africa, Asia, and Latin America" in Havana, participants allegedly made plans to undermine American society through drug trafficking and other criminal activity.[6] A few years later, a Drug Enforcement Administration (DEA) intelligence document reported that the Cuban embassies in Canada and Mexico were regularly facilitating heroin trafficking into the United States.[7]

In 1975, Cuba's "narco-state" activities began. It started when Colombian vessels carrying cocaine destined for the United States strayed into Cuban waters. The Cubans searched and seized many of these ships, confiscating their cargoes and imprisoning their crews. The drug lords and the Cuban Ambassador to Colombia Fernando Ravelo-Renedo, then held a secret meeting in Bogotá to discuss the release of the Colombian merchandise and crews. The result of the meeting was astonishing: not only would Cuba not intervene further in Colombian drug trafficking, but it would also provide fuel, ports, and repair services. Cuba also offered escorts in and out of ports and Cuban flags to disguise the vessels' origin, all at the price of $800,000 per vessel.[8] Even Cuban air space came up for sale.[9] The Cuban-Colombian relationship went further. Drug traffickers now helped Cuba smuggle arms into Colombia to support the M-19, a Colombian insurgent organization. The narco-insurgent relationship was taking shape.

The capture in Mexico of a key player in the Cuban-Colombian drugs-for-arms operation, Jaime Guillot-Lara, subsequently proved this relationship. Unfortunately, Mexican authorities released Guillot-Lara and he escaped to Spain; but key witnesses David Lorenzo Perez (Guillot-Lara's connection), Johnny Crump (Colombian lawyer and drug dealer), and Mario Esteves Gonzales (Cuban intelligence agent) provided evidence to the grand jury in Miami in the Guillot-Lara case in February 1983.[10] According to their testimonies, Guillott-Lara's shipments left Colombia flying a Cuban flag to identify them as friendly to Cuba. The Cuban navy would then escort these boats to the Cuban Keys where Cuban intelligence officers transferred the drugs to smaller boats. These boats then trafficked the drugs into United

States waters.

Guillot-Lara's operations had gone awry when he attempted to deliver seven tons of arms to the M-19 in return for 8,000 pounds of marijuana. After the plane carrying the arms was ditched during the flight, authorities found the plane and the Colombian army captured the arms from the M-19. In their evidence, M-19 guerrillas implicated the Cuban embassy as sources of recruitment and training, and as a result Colombia expelled Cuban Ambassador Ravelo-Renedo and his staff. Colombian authorities later sank one of Guillot-Lara's seaborne arms shipments on the Colombian Pacific coast and impounded another. It was at this point that Guillot-Lara fled to Mexico, where Mexican authorities subsequently captured him.[11]

Perez also testified that Cuba had received $800,000 in profits from smuggling methaqualone tablets, and 30 percent of profits from the sale of 23,000 pounds of marijuana, both sold in the United States. Esteves testified that his task had been to distribute cocaine, marijuana, and methaqualone in the United States, and that within a fifteen-month period he had delivered $2 to $3 million to his Cuban supervisors. Esteves also testified before the New York State Select Committee that Castro was personally involved in drug trafficking. He stated that Castro's goals included promoting violent crime, drug addiction, and corruption in North America, and, furthermore, that the mass deportation of criminals from Cuba to Florida in 1980 had provided cover for introducing a network of drug trafficking agents into the United States.[12] Two months later, before a Joint Senate Committee, Tom Boyatt, former United States Ambassador to Colombia, testified that

> . . .the Guillot-Lara case proves that the drug trafficking structure, the same people, the same plans, the same means of transportation, were used to carry marijuana northward to hurt the United States and to bring guns south to Colombia to supply the M-19 for the purpose of overthrowing the freely elected government of Colombia, and that is a matter of evidence and record.[13]

The evidence that Cuba is playing a key role in hemispheric drug trafficking is abundant. The infamous drug lord Carlos Ledher Rivas operated from Cuba during the time that the Colombian government was applying heavy pressure on drug traffickers. Ledher, who after his arrest boasted that "coca has been transformed into a revolutionary weapon for the struggle against American imperialism,"[14] testified before a United States federal court about personal meetings with Raul Castro to discuss illegal drug movements through Cuba. At this stage, President Ronald Reagan had heard enough. He authorized a "sting" operation in which DEA agents would pose as drug smugglers to coordinate a secret meeting with the Cuban Interior Minister Jose Abrahantes (whose office was suspected of running the drug operations) aboard a yacht at sea, and make the arrest. However, a double agent alerted Cuban authorities to the operation, which was carried out under the Bush administration, and Abrahantes broke off the meeting in May 1989.[15]

Feeling the pressure from Washington, and not wanting to become a Manuel Noriega predecessor (Noriega, at that time president of Panama, was becoming increasingly unpopular with American officialdom for his drug-smuggling activities and would be ousted in December of 1989) Castro arrested a number of senior Cuban military officials in July 1989 and charged them with drug trafficking. Among those arrested were Cuban war hero Major General Arnaldo Ochoa Sanchez, Colonel Antonio de la Guardia, Major Amado Padron, and Captain Jorge Martinez. General Ochoa, though popular with the nation, was not favored by Castro. Ochoa advocated a decentralized economy and was leaning away from a single-party rule for Cuba. As part of the Cuban drug smuggling operations, he was an easy sacrifice for Castro. Ochoa and the other three were executed in July 1989.

Brigadier General Patricio de la Guardia, Antonio's brother, was imprisoned along with several others. Patricio was accused of smuggling African ivory to Cuba while on duty in Angola. Patricio admitted to sending Castro two elephant tusks for his birthday. His real crime, however, may have been the fact that he had knowledge of his brother's involvement in the Cuban state-run drug smuggling activities. According to Patricio, Antonio's involvement in drug smuggling was deep, but all under the direction of the Cuban Interior Minister. In fact, on the same day as the arrest, Antonio informed Patricio that he (Antonio) had personally delivered $3 million from the latest drug operation to Abrahantes. The minister congratulated Antonio and ordered him to obtain $12 million more before the end of the year.[16]

Recently, the exiled daughter of Antonio de la Guardia filed a complaint against Castro in a French court, accusing him of drug trafficking and hoping to clear her father's name. Ileana de la Guardia told reporters at the Palais de Justice that Cuban drug smuggling "was a matter of state, organized at the highest echelons of the power in the country."[17] Even one of Castro's own daughters, Alina Fernández, reveals in her book, *Castro's Daugher: An Exile's Memoir of Cuba,* Fidel's trafficking of illegal drugs. At one point she states: "How do you think Latin American guerrillas paid for their arms supply? With cocaine!" She also tells of the friends she lost because of the Ochoa case.

Jorge Cabrera, arrested by U.S. authorities and given a 19-year prison sentence for smuggling cocaine, has also accused Cuban authorities of drug smuggling. Upon his arrest, a photograph of Cabrera with Castro was found among his possessions. Cabrera claimed to have worked directly with high-ranking Cuban officials and Cali Cartel figure Carlos Tascon, a major shipper of United States-bound drugs through Cuban waters. He offered to work undercover in exchange for a reduced prison sentence, but the Justice Department believed his story was self-serving and not credible.[18] This inaction prompted Cabrera's lawyer, Stephen Bronis, to charge that the federal government did nothing to verify Cabrera's claim. Bronis initially wanted his client to say nothing of the Cuban involvement for his own protection, but Cabrera insisted. Bronis, whose own private investigation supports Cabrera's claims, wrote to United States Attorney General Janet Reno requesting an investigation.

Castro's other drug smuggling activities are said to include mediation services between top Colombian drug lords and Panama's General Manuel Noriega. Panamanian forces captured and destroyed a key drug lab while Noriega was out of the country. Castro apparently coordinated Panama's release of the 23 Colombians arrested in that operation, the return of some lab equipment to the traffickers, and the return of $3 million in cash to the cartel.[19] Meetings for these arrangements allegedly took place in Havana.

According to knowledgeable analysts, Castro also supported drug lord Pablo Escobar's operations in return for financial aid to the M-19 guerrillas operating in Colombia. Part of this assistance included providing Cuban air force aircraft for Escobar's travels to Nicaragua,[20] which Escobar used as an intermediary staging base for drug shipments from Colombia to the United States.

Over the past decade, Castro has claimed a willingness to support the fight against the drug war, sentiments which he expresses even today. Although some of his activities appear to be sincere, the reason, in part, could be economic. Cuba has not received the economic assistance it once received from the Soviet Union. Castro has a greater need to promote good will rather than revolution in order to ensure respectability among his democratic North American and Latin American neighbors, respectability that he apparently hopes will turn into investments.[21] With the Cuban economy in dire straits, Castro's motivation is at best questionable. Even as early as 1984, before Communism took its fall, former DEA Chief Francis Mullen stated before a House Committee on Foreign Affairs, Task Force on International Drug Trafficking:

> The Cubans apparently deal only with those drug smugglers they trust or those who can provide some benefit or service to Cuba such as smuggling weapons, as illustrated in the Guillot investigation. Cuba

continues to seize vessels and aircraft carrying drug cargo into its territories that do not have necessary official contacts in Cuba.[22]

Washington first noted Nicaragua's involvement when pilot Barry Seal, working undercover for the DEA, needed a halfway refueling point in order to carry a large amount of cocaine from Colombia destined for the United States. The location chosen was Nicaragua, where Fredico Vaughan, a senior official of Nicaragua's interior ministry, met him. Seal's operation provided photographs showing both Vaughan and Escobar at the Nicaraguan military airstrip.[23] A year later, in 1985, another agent, James Herring, whose testimony led to nine arrests and convictions, implicated Vaughan and his boss, Interior Minister Tomas Borges, in a drug-smuggling ring. These events provided information on the Sandinista involvement in processing and shipping cocaine to the United States, which included using official Nicaraguan planes and diplomatic couriers to smuggle cocaine from Colombia and Bolivia to processing laboratories in Managua. Herring also confirmed that Borges and Vaughan were in charge of the operations.[24]

Several Nicaraguan defectors supported Herring's testimony and explained Nicaragua's "moral" and "political" justifications for the drug trafficking. Former Nicaraguan diplomat Antonio Farach detailed one meeting between Sandinista defense minister Humberto Ortega, brother of former president Daniel Ortega, and Raul Castro, Fidel Castro's brother, in which they discussed the establishment of the narco-trafficking infrastructure in Nicaragua. When Farach questioned this, his superiors told him:

> In the first place, drugs did not remain in Nicaragua; the drugs were destined for the United States. Our youth would not be harmed, but rather the youth of our enemies. Therefore, the drugs were used as a political weapon against the United States. The drug trafficking produced a very good economic benefit which we needed for our revolution. We wanted to provide food to our people with the suffering and death of the youth of the United States.[25]

Alvaro Baldizon, another defector who worked for the Borges interior ministry, provided similar testimony. He said Borges had explained to him that Nicaragua's drug trafficking had three objectives: corrupting and destroying America's youth, thereby undermining America's strength; using American youth to finance liberation movements; and using the narco-trafficking network to smuggle arms bought on the black market.[26]

Using drugs as a weapon in attempting to destroy a society is not a new strategy. The Japanese used such a strategy against the Chinese just prior to the Sino-Japanese War in 1937 and during World War II. The Japanese and Chinese had been enemies for centuries. Aware of the social destruction that drugs cause, as well as the devastating role that opium had played in China since the 18th century,[27] the Japanese distributed opium and heroin along the China coast when they took control of Manchuria in 1931, earning $300 million per year.[28] The strategy not only helped finance Japan's war machine, but the Japanese planners thought that it would make the subsequent occupation of China much easier because drug-consumption would reduce the combat effectiveness of Chinese troops. Japanese wartime occupation authorities distributed as much opium, heroin, and cocaine as possible: they paid employees with drugs, opened clinics to provide drugs, and reinstated poppy farms. Koreans were put in charge of the illegal drug operations to ensure no Japanese agents risked addiction. The Japanese also used this strategy during their cruel occupation of Nanking. "To encourage addiction and further enslave the people, the Japanese routinely used narcotics as payment for labor and prostitution in Nanking," writes author Iris Chang. "Heroin cigarettes were offered to children as young as ten."[29] Ironically, the addiction problem increased crime dramatically in the city, rather than decreasing it, souring the current argument that legalizing drugs would decrease the crime rate. It took the iron fist of communism, amongst other things, to finally pull China from its drug-ridden lifestyle.[30]

But in the Western Hemisphere, it was Cuba that used drugs as a weapon with the United States as the target and Fidel Castro the operational architect. He was a leader in establishing bonds and strengthening relationships with the cartels, Latin American guerrilla groups, the Sandinista regime, and even Panamanian Dictator Noriega. But narco-terrorism was only just beginning. It would grow to enormous proportions in Peru and Colombia.

Peru: It Grew to Narco-Terrorism

Atrocity was standard procedure for Peru's Shining Path guerrillas, and its methods of killing were usually brutal. The example of Maria Elena Moyano was typical. When she was elected vice mayor of a small Peruvian villa shantytown at age 33, Moyano had worked hard to transform this impoverished community. She had been a volunteer teacher and founded the town's women's organization. On an early summer day, the town had gathered for a neighborhood barbecue feast. Moyano had organized the gathering to raise money for the community's needy children. As citizens ate barbecue together, gunfire and screams suddenly broke the calm. A group of Shining Path terrorists armed with pistols and hand grenades pushed through the crowd. Moyano tried to step away but a woman standing next to her pulled out a pistol and shot her. Other terrorists joined in and filled her full of bullets. They grabbed her by the hair and dragged her into the open, stuffed dynamite under her body and disappeared just before the massive explosion tore Moyano's body apart.[31]

The Shining Path has been guilty of numerous atrocities such as bombings; disfiguring peasant voters; destroying crops, livestock and development projects; using machetes to hack babies to death in front of their mothers; severing children's ears for being patients at State-run hospitals; and, on one occasion, forcing each person of a village to cut a piece of flesh off the bodies of live nuns until the nuns died.

The Shining Path's founder, philosophy professor Abimael Guzman, launched the movement at the University of Huamanga in Ayacucho in 1970. Advocating an extreme interpretation of the orthodox philosophy of China's Mao Tse Tung,[32] the Shining Path early adopted a policy of extreme brutality against anyone who opposed its revolution, ultimately killing 30,000 civilians, displacing another 600,000,[33] and leaving more than 131,700 children orphans.[34] Its war on Peruvian institutions has had a devastating impact on the country.

The Shining Path's brutality was recognized internationally, and as a result the movement had no political allies and received no outside support, unlike most other terrorist-insurgent organizations. Mao's China always disavowed the Shining Path. The organization lacked connections to other Communist regimes such as Vietnam, North Korea, Cuba, or the Soviet Union.[35] The group, therefore, found drug-trafficking activities in the Upper Huallaga regions a productive source of income to finance its insurgent operations based on terrorism.[36] The Shining Path did not get directly involved in the drug trade, however, but rather levied a tax on cultivation and movement of coca and accepted substantial contributions in money and arms from drug traffickers to combat Peruvian army and police or United States DEA interference.[37]

The Shining Path's involvement in the drug business seems to have begun unintentionally. In the 1980s, the Shining Path moved quietly into the Upper Huallaga Valley. At this time, the United States was pressuring the Peruvian government to do more about the cocaine problem. Peru sent special counter-narcotics units to destroy coca farms, and also sought to establish other programs to eliminate coca from the Upper Huallaga. This alienated the farmers, who saw their government and the United States destroying what little livelihood they had. The Shining Path exploited that resentment by protecting the farmers from these counter-narcotic units, and thus a convenient relationship began between the Shining Path and the peasants.

Many peasants did not really know, or care, about the ideological goals of the Shining Path, but wanted only protection for their coca farms.[38]

But the Shining Path's involvement in the drug trade began in earnest as a result of a second phase in this guerrilla-peasant relationship. Colombian cocaine dealers had run the coca businesses in the Upper Huallaga Valley prior to the arrival of the Shining Path. These wealthy Colombian drug barons were able to purchase the most modern weapons and communications equipment and maintain their own paramilitary forces. They bribed or coerced local officials into cooperating with them. The drug lords paid the growers well, but any farmer who could not produce his portion, even if it was because of government eradication programs, was routinely executed as both a reprisal and a warning. A similar fate came to those who chose not to grow coca at all. When the Shining Path entered the region and put a stop to the counter-narcotics government programs, it also ended the Colombian abuses. Inevitably, this increased the Shining Path's involvement in the drug trade. The peasants still needed to sell their coca, so, as the Shining Path began protecting the growers, they also began collecting a subsidy from Colombian drug traffickers for protecting airstrips from the Peruvian government. This latter activity resulted in a closer working relationship with the Colombian drug lords, thus establishing the bond in the Peruvian-Colombian narco-terrorism marriage and providing finances for the Shining Path.[39] At the same time, the Shining Path protected the drug trade from Peruvian and United States government efforts. By controlling and providing security at numerous narco-trafficking landing strips, the Shining Path collected between $6,000 and $15,000 per flight.[40]

In 1993, Peruvian narco-traffickers made an estimated net profit of $700 million.[41] How much of this went to the Shining Path can only be estimated. Several Pentagon officials believe the amount to be quite small. However, considering the interwoven relationship between the players, the sum could be quite large. The United States Government Accounting Office estimates the amount to be between $10 to $100 million.[42] In fact, with 60 percent of the world's coca being produced in Peru during the 1980s and early 1990s, profits from Peru's drug trade were so lucrative that the Shining Path was fighting another, smaller Peruvian terrorist organization, the Tupac Amaru Revolutionary Movement (MRTA), for control of coca-growing areas.[43]

From the outset the MRTA financed its operations through narco-trafficking.[44] This group controlled the town of Yurimaguas and the surrounding areas in the northern part of the Upper Huallaga Valley, but eventually dissolved due to its own weak leadership and the overbearing strength of the Shining Path. However, with the decline of the Shining Path's power in the early 1990s, the MRTA seemed to be making a comeback. It was the MRTA that held the hostages at the Japanese ambassador's residence in 1996.

In the 1980s, the Peruvian government tried to handle this insurgent-drug problem as two separate issues instead of formulating a single strategy against narco-terrorism. It did so in part because of the legitimate fear that the United States would not allow its aid to be channeled to Peru's internal guerrilla struggle. However, there also existed a rivalry between the Peruvian police and military. Each comes under a different government ministry and, therefore, each has a different mission. While police fought the drugs, the military fought terrorism, and operations proceeded separately. Economic problems led to severe cuts in military budgets accompanied by salary reductions, but the police departments received supplementary funding from Washington as part of a joint United States-Peruvian anti-drug effort. Disaster resulted. The police and military never shared intelligence and other pertinent information. Each government-declared emergency zone had to be under control of the police or the Army, not both, which enhanced the narco-terrorists' freedom of maneuver.[45] The Shining Path easily fought off the police while the drug barons bribed the ill-paid military personnel. At one point, the military failed to support the police during a large-scale Shining Path assault on a major police station in the city of Uchiza. The station fell. The insurgents then took control of the city and executed every surviving police officer.[46] The result of this narco-terrorist relationship was a terrorist-run state within Peru's borders (the Upper Huallaga Valley), which signified an embarrassing loss of sovereignty for the Peruvian democratic government.

In mid-1989, however, the Peruvian military began its most successful counter-insurgency campaign and pushed the Shining Path out of most of the Upper Huallaga Valley in seven months. In November 1989, military authorities celebrated Armed Forces Day in the main square of Uchiza, the same city the Shining Path had captured the preceding March. But the victory was short lived. The Commanding General of the Army decided to use drug money for his poorly budgeted military to accomplish his campaign, a decision that branded him in the eyes of the Peruvian and American authorities. The result was that the general in command was relieved and within one year the Shining Path regained control of the Upper Huallaga Valley.[47]

Elected (now former) President Alberto Fujimori, in 1990, grasped the complexity of the narco-terrorism relationship and also recognized the economic side of the problem—alternate development assistance for the coca-growing *compesinos*. Fujimori made his perception clear to Washington when he rejected $35.9 million in anti-drug military assistance. Without proper security in the coca-growing areas of the Upper Huallaga Valley, he explained, his government could not implement economic development programs. In 1991 he reached an agreement with Washington on "the need to feed, equip, train, provide uniforms, and adequately support the armed and police forces who will be fighting against narcotrafficking *and those who support and encourage it* [italics added]."[48]

Fujimori's strategy was very successful. Guzman, the Shining Path leader, was captured, and the insurgency began to disintegrate. Without the security of the Shining Path, Colombian traffickers found the operation too risky. Peru's governmental authorities installed eradication and alternate development programs. As a center of drug production, Peru, once a major player in the drug trade, began to decline in significance.

In the past couple of years, however, coca-growing rose again as a primary crop for many *compesinos*, and the Shining Path are re-emerging. There are several reasons for the revival of both. For one, the Peruvian military and police were required to disperse their efforts, responding, among other things, to border tensions with Ecuador. After the September 11 attacks, the Shining Path, claiming to see the United States as a vulnerable nation no longer capable of fighting terrorism, also took advantage of the diminished Peruvian internal security and began putting its forces back together.

But the drug reproduction began again even before the Shining Path's re-emergence. President Fujimori pointed out the reason as being the "cyclical nature" of drug production, which is "unavoidably tied to the appetite for cocaine in America and Europe."[49] And there is the permanent problem of financial attraction of coca production to a rural population mired in poverty. "Coca is the only resource we have to make a living," one peasant put it. "There just isn't enough work for all of us."[50] Still, one thing was clear—by fighting the drug traffickers and the guerrillas as a single entity (narco-terrorists) Peru was able to eliminate much its terrorism and drug problems. This success forced the Colombian drug lords to find a new place in which to grow their coca—their own country.

Colombia: A Narco-Terrorist "Superstate"

On November 6, 1985, Colombia grabbed worldwide headlines when M-19 guerrillas seized the Colombian Palace of Justice, in Bogotá, and took 250 hostages, ninety-five of whom they killed, including eleven of the twenty-four justices. In time, it became apparent that the guerrillas conducted the attack to intimidate the justices into declaring the extradition treaty of drug lords to the United States illegal, for in the three months prior to this event the justices had received numerous death threats and bribes to overrule the treaty. The guerillas burned extradition files during the seizure[51] and reportedly received $1 million from the Medellín Cartel for the attack.[52]

Acts of terrorism by the powerful drug lords of the 1980s and early 1990s were common, as judges and other government officials were forced to accept bribes or be killed if they did not rule in favor of captured drug traffickers. Between 1985 and 1993, Colombian narco-terrorists assassinated over 1,000 public officials, twelve Supreme Court justices, more than fifty judges, over 170 other judicial employees, a narcotics police chief, an attorney general, and three presidential candidates. They even murdered journalists, including a major newspaper publisher, for their anti-drug stance. In 1989, the late Pablo Escobar ordered the bombing of a domestic airliner, killing all 107 passengers. Such terrorism forced Colombia to eventually relinquish its extradition efforts with the United States. Carlos Mauro Hoyo, while serving as the Colombian Attorney General, called the narco-terrorist relationship in his country a drug "superstate," and soon afterward the M-19 guerrillas assassinated him.[53] Hoyo, of course, was correct.

But with the eventual break up of the major drug cartels, the guerrillas took greater control of the illegal drug trade. The narco-trafficker/guerrilla relationship existed in Colombia as early as the 1980s. The three primary insurgent groups in that country were the Armed Revolutionary Forces of Colombia (FARC), the Army of National Liberation (ELN), and the April 19 Movement (M-19),[54] all of which began supporting the narco-traffickers by providing security for drug-smuggling operations. The most prominent of these in Colombia, if not the world, is the FARC. Throughout the 1970s, a time of surplus and growth for most socialist insurgencies, the FARC had great difficulty in making ends meet and could barely maintain a strength of 100 guerrillas. However, by the mid-1980s it had grown into a force of over 2000 guerrillas and additional support of more than 5000 political cadres. This sudden increase resulted from only one thing—drugs.[55] So vital to FARC's existence were drugs that in May 1984, when a government commission met with FARC leaders in the Alto de la Mesa rain forest to negotiate peace, the effort failed because the two sides could not reach an agreement on a cessation of drug-trafficking. The Colombian government agreed to consider amnesty for various FARC members, instituted political and land reforms, and provided loans to assist FARC members in returning to civilian life. But the FARC command was unwilling to give up the substantial income it received from protecting coca-growers, while the Colombian government, pressured by the United States, would not stop its counter-drug campaign.[56]

Today the guerrillas actively grow, process, and transport illegal drugs. Revenues for Colombian terrorists come from the sale of cocaine, marijuana,[57] and heroin. Throughout the late 1990s it was estimated that 80 percent of the world's cocaine came from Colombia.[58] Today it can be estimated at 65-70 percent, with the rest coming from Peru and Bolivia. Colombia also provides about half of the heroin consumed in the United States, most of which is used in the highly populated Eastern part of the country. Heroin production in Colombia went from zero to 6.5 metric tones in five years in the early 1990s, and helped create an additional 100,000 addicts in the United States from 1994 to 1997.[59] As a result of drug trafficking, the guerrillas netted substantial funds. According to the Colombian Military Command, the guerrillas obtained more than $746 million from drug trafficking activities in 1996.[60] Colombian Defense Minister Echeverri publicly asserted that the FARC and ELN earned a combined total of about $900 million dollars in 1997,[61] of which a more moderate $500 million came from drug activity.[62] The United States General Accounting Office estimates the FARC and ELN earn $600 million a year from the drug trade.[63] "I think the earnings of the guerrillas could be about $1 million to $2 million a day," Colombian President Andrés Pastrana declared in February 2000.[64]

While Colombia's narco-terrorist relationship grew significantly in the 1990s, so did war. In 1997 Colombia accounted for 83.6 percent of all terrorist incidents in Latin America with 107 reported acts of terrorism.[65] According to one estimate, approximately ten Colombians die every day as a result of political violence.[66] Another source provides a similar number at 3,500 deaths per year.[67] The guerrillas commonly used terrorist methods, including the slaughter of farmers and peasants, to gain control of rural regions in Colombia.[68] More recent tactics have been become even more brutal. One such case included the massacre of more than over two dozen farmers with machetes, and raping at least one woman.[69]

Also during 1997 the insurgents caused enormous havoc in municipal elections. They gave mayoral candidates three days to quit the election race or face death. All thirty-one candidates withdrew. The rebels also used kidnapping, murder and terrorist threats to pressure more than 1,120 mayor and council candidates in 125 different municipalities to cease efforts to run for office. The guerrillas killed some twenty-three candidates while 130 more were abducted and threatened or lectured on the evils of their campaigns.[70]

In early August 1998, the FARC and ELN[71] launched a massive offensive and the Colombian army experienced one of its biggest defeats in its counter-insurgency experience. The rebels struck more than forty-five times in a matter of days across the entire country, targeting oil pipelines, hydro-electric dams, and numerous military and police bases. The most devastating attack was on the Miraflores counter-narcotics base, which the United States had supported heavily. The FARC hit the base with rockets, mortars, and large-caliber weapons, eventually overrunning it and capturing or killing as many as 200 police and military personnel.[72] The FARC launched an offensive against more than twenty towns including one only twenty-five miles from Bogotá, and destroyed bridges and power stations. This attack compelled emergency meetings between Washington and the Colombian government. It also prompted the former Office of National Drug Control Policy director Barry McCraffey, who clearly understood the depth of the "narc-FARC" connection, to request $1 billion in aid to Colombia to bolster its war on drugs—a measure which later became part of the Colombia Plan.[73]

Attacks by the FARC gave them so much leverage that President Pastrana agreed to withdraw military and police personnel from an area of Colombian territory larger than Connecticut, Massachusetts, and Rhode Island combined. This territory—the "Demilitarized Zone"—is now turning into a FARC haven for furthering both insurgent and drug trafficking operations. The guerrillas train new recruits, plan future attacks, hold hostages, and trade drugs for arms within their new state.[74] Colombia's neighbors worried that the war would spill over the Colombian borders, and it has. "If the process of advances in terrorism continues," former Peruvian President Fujimori has declared, "it will constitute, I don't have the least doubt, a threat to the continent."[75] Colombian rebels are already known to be crossing into Ecuador, Panama, and possibly Brazil.

Obviously, the Colombian guerrillas were able to transform themselves into one of the most powerful insurgencies ever in Latin America, one capable of dealing effectively with the Colombian army.

The narco-terrorists, like any official state agency, have developed foreign policy instruments including force, economic leverage, propaganda, and diplomacy. This immense power has seriously undermined Colombia's ability to maintain law and order.

This success brought the Pastrana administration to the negotiation table, but as the peace talks focused mostly on the larger and more powerful FARC, it led the ELN to increase its terrorist activities in order to gain a greater voice in the settlements, and its own demilitarized zone. At one point the ELN even hijacked and abducted forty-one passengers on a Colombian airline, and kidnapped almost a hundred churchgoers the following month.

The latter kidnapping was of major interest because it occurred in a wealthy section of a major city, Cali. The rebels, who control much of the country-side, had not yet been so bold as to go into a prominent urban center and abduct scores of people from a church during a mid-morning mass. A hot pursuit by military forces did result in the liberation of all but twenty of the hostages.[76]

An additional terrorist organization is also making its presence felt dur-ing the peace negotiations—the non-government right-wing paramilitaries called the United Self-Defense Groups of Colombia (AUC). This group, num-bering 5,000 in size, developed in 1985 from a small group of armed peasant farmers gathered by two brothers to avenge the killing of their father by the FARC. The AUC are blamed for many of the country's worst atrocities, including mass killings of villagers supportive of the insurgents.[77] In January of 1999 the AUC swept through six provinces hunting down FARC and ELN supporters. According to the U.S. State Department's country report on human rights in Colombia, "Paramilitary groups murdered, tortured, and threatened civilians suspected of sympathizing with the guerrillas...."[78] In May, 1999, the AUC abducted Colombian Senator and human-rights activist Piedad Cordoba as a "message of peace." That "message" meant providing the AUC the same political status that Pastrana provided the leftist guerrillas during the peace process.[79] These challenges by the ELN and the AUC prove that negotiating with terrorists is a losing cause. By providing legitimacy to the FARC, Pastrana legitimizes violence, thereby encouraging further vio-lence by the ELN and AUC.

Right-wing paramilitary groups are particularly active in the banana region of Urbana. As banana plantations expanded, so did the number of plantation laborers. But as the drug market increased in the area, the trafTick-ers made deals with the paramilitaries to drive off the banana workers to make room for more coca farms, and the region became the ground of a ruthless power struggle between the guerrillas and paramilitaries trying to gain ultimate control of the coca-growing territory, with the army fighting against both. Official 1995 figures showed that 1,258 innocent people died in Urbana that year, 200 of them in mass slaughters. Over 25,000 refugees have fled the war zone.[80]

One calamitous by-product of the fighting among the insurgents, paramilitaries, and government forces during the past several years has been the massive population displacement. The official estimate is that approxi-mately 1.4 million Colombians were refugees in their own land by 1999. That almost equals the population of the state of West Virginia. Approxi-mately 308,000 people became displaced in 1998 alone. In some cases entire populations of towns took to flight *en masse*, the largest exodus consisting of 10,000 people. The guerrillas and paramilitaries use whatever means necessary, including torture and murder, to force people to flee their homes. In addition to the hundreds of thousands of refugees who remain in Colombia, more than 180,000 live in refugee-like circumstances in Venezuela, Ecuador, and Panama.[81]

Violence is likely to continue despite the peace negotiations. In fact, assaults by the FARC and ELN increased 148 percent in 1999.[82] Fostering political instability is important to the Colombian drug lords, as this allows drug trafficking to flow under less scrutiny and with less resistance. According to one Colombian authority, Colombian drug syndicates apparently financed both sides of a long-standing civil conflict in Burundi (Africa) to ensure instability. They rearmed the Hutu extremists who carried out genocidal raids in Tutsi-controlled Rwanda, while they also funded arm sales to the Tutsi extremists. Hundreds of thousands of civilians were murdered by both sides in this war. The goal of the cartel, according to a former Burundi foreign minister, was to "maintain turmoil so that large drug shipments, mainly cocaine, [could] move freely through Burundi to other destinations."[83]

From the above example, one can conclude that even though the Colombian government strives to reach a peace agreement with the insurgents, it is to the advantage of the narco-traffickers that fighting and turmoil continue, as instability enables narco-trafficking to flow much more freely. Therefore, major drug traffickers are now financing not only the leftist insurgents, but also their right-wing enemy the AUC. In 1999, a major government police operation destroyed a large drug laboratory run by the paramilitaries. The lab was capable of producing eight tons of cocaine per month.[84] Today AUC leader Carlos Castano claims that the his organization derives 70 percent of its funding from the illegal drug business. This narco-terrorist relationship with the AUC has increased AUC strength and operational abilities against the FARC and ELN, thereby intensifying the fighting and causing further strain on the insurgent-government peace negotiations, such as happened in Burundi. As long as the drug lords can fuel the ability of the insurgents and paramilitaries to fight, peace is not likely.[85]

Colombian narco-terrorists have even formed alliances with crime syndicates in the former U.S.S.R., which acquire cocaine for distribution and in turn provide weapons to Latin American dealers. According to one source:

> Intelligence agencies of Colombia and the United States have detected an unusual increase of ships under Russian flag that, in most

cases, go to Turbo (Antioquia) to unload arsenals and set sail again loaded with cocaine, heroin, and marijuana.

The weapons, especially cargoes of Russian AK-47s and fragmentation grenades, are sold to the highest bidder among paramilitaries, guerrillas, and drug traffickers.[86]

These Russian groups have been operating out of Miami, New York, and Puerto Rico and are extremely competent, dangerous and sophisticated. "We are talking about people with PhDs, former senior KGB agents, with sophisticated weapons, people who have [already] laundered billions of dollars," one Russian expert in the DEA stated.[87] They recently provided Colombian drug dealers with million-dollar helicopters and surface-to-air-missiles. They even contemplated providing the Colombian drug lords with a Russian submarine, complete with crew and a former Soviet admiral.[88] In September 2000, the Colombian drug traffickers almost had their submarine when officials discovered the vessel under construction with the assistance of both Russian and American engineers. This submarine could have carried up to 200 tons of cocaine.[89]

Perhaps the most frightening recent developments in Colombia involve the FARC's growing international connections. On August 11, 2001 three leading figures of the Irish Republican Army (IRA) were arrested in Colombia. Two of these men were experts in explosives, and one was a key figure with close relations to the Cuban government.[90] The men were arrested in Bogotá after returning from San Vicente de Caguan, the heart of FARC held territory, and the same location, coincidentally, of an Iranian invested "meatpacking" plant. While such an enterprise is a viable economic stimulus for the territory, the Colombian military appears to have doubts about its authenticity. Colombian Defense Minister Luis Fernando Ramirez, who believes the Iranians are working as advisors to the FARC, stated the Iranian workers going to the plant have resisted inspection of their bags.[91] As of this writing, this meatpacking plant has not been established.

But for the most powerful insurgency in the history of South America to request advisors from the Middle East makes one ask: advice for what? Perhaps the connection will assist expanding Colombian drug trafficking to new markets, with Iran obtaining some of the proceeds. However, perhaps of greater concern is Iran's current chemical weapons build-up via a Chinese company: Yongli Chemical.[92] Are some of these chemicals finding their way to FARC controlled territory in Colombia? The FARC is a powerful force to be taken seriously. The idea of using their support to produce weapons of mass destruction within the Western Hemisphere is not far-fetched. The

FARC are known to have ties with the Iranian-backed Hizbollah, and that they may be strengthening ties with other "Jihad" forces is not unrealistic. Most likely, the IRA and Iranian contacts will be receiving revenues from the lucrative drug trade for their services.

Other Locations of Narco-Terrorism

The Golden Crescent and Muslim Extremists

In the early 1990s, Pakistan became prominent for the high production of poppy, to produce opium and heroin, within its borders. During this time India alleged that Pakistan, its bitter enemy, consciously promoted the narcotics trade in order to fund terrorism within India and to damage the fabric of Indian society.[93] Indian Prime Minister Narashimha Rio claimed that narco-terrorism was contributing substantially to his country's instability, and was threatening India's economic reforms.[94]

But by the mid-1990s Pakistan's drug eradication efforts had successfully decreased opium poppy production in their country. However, not unlike the pattern of counterdrug efforts in South America, the drugs did not disappear, and Pakistani counterdrug efforts merely resulted in much of the poppy fields and opium labs moving across the border into Afghanistan. In the past five years Afghanistan has produced more than 70 percent of the global opium supply, 90 percent of which is smuggled into Europe.[95] Just like other places in the world, there was a military movement willing to take advantage of the incoming profit from illegal drug trafficking—the Taliban. As the Taliban movement began its takeover of the country, it developed a close relationship with major Afghani drug lords who supplied the Taliban with revenues from the drug trade and weapons to further the Taliban cause, and in return received security and a safe haven to produce opiates. As the Taliban's war grew, so did its relationship with the drug traffickers, until the two developed a symbiotic relationship. By 2001, the Taliban controlled 96% of the territory where poppy was grown, and was estimated to be making about $50 million from their opiate proceeds,[96] making up about 55 percent of the Taliban's budget.[97] Not quite the astonishing $600 million the Colombian guerillas make, but still a significant amount to finance an army in such a poverty-stricken country. In fact, in 1999 when much of the heroin was being smuggled through Iran, the *New York Times* wrote that Iranian authorities claimed:

> . . . heavy machine guns mounted on all-terrain vehicles often protect drug convoys, while traffickers themselves are sometimes armed with rocket-propelled grenades or mortars. Iranian officials say that some

groups have shot down Iranian helicopters and warplanes with surface-to-air weapons. . . .[98]

The amount the world-renowned terrorist, Osama Bin Laden, who currently operates from Afghanistan, obtains directly from the Southwest heroin drug trade for his terrorist activities is not believed to be significant, at the time of this writing. Bin Laden obviously has close ties to the Taliban and some high-ranking drug lords. In fact, the Taliban's leader, Mullah Omar, is even believed to be an in-law of Bin Laden's (via marriage to one of Bin Laden's daughters). Yet, at the time of this writing there is no clear evidence that Bin Laden, or his terrorist network, Al Qaeda, makes significant amounts of money from the Afghani drug trade. It is possible that Bin Laden or Al Qaeda do have some investments in the Afghan opium and heroin trade, but it is likely the majority of funding for their terrorist activities on a strategic level comes from outside support, such as anti-American Muslim States.

Interestingly, some Al Qaeda members may be making a profit from drug trafficking in South America. Currently, the Bush Administration is collecting evidence of Al Qaeda cocaine trafficking operatives working on the Paraguay-Argentina-Brazil border.[99] This tri-nation border area is home to a large Muslim population, and it is believed that Islamic terrorist organizations associated with Al Qaeda and Iran's Party of God, such as the Lebanese Hezbollah and the Egyptian Islamic Jihad, amongst others, operate in this tri-border area.

Al Qaeda members are also believed to produce terrorist funds from drugs right in the U.S. Amin Mohamed Ahmed, of Yemen, is currently wanted by U.S. Customs for the manufacture and sale of methamphetamines, a very dangerous and addictive form of narcotic, which is becoming one of America's most dangerous drug threats. Ahmed is believed to be an associate of Osama Bin Laden and responsible for raising funds for terrorist acts. It is feasible that numerous small terrorist cells in the U.S. (such as the Al Qaeda "sleeper" cells) could support themselves with local drug dealing.

In the summer of 2001, the Taliban destroyed most of the poppy production in their territories and made production of opium illegal within their territory. Considering the beneficial Taliban/drug lord relationship in Afghanistan, this development seems strange, but it is easily explained. While poppy fields were destroyed and production was made illegal, distribution and sale of opiates remained legal. Why? So much poppy was being produced in Afghanistan that the price of Southwest Asian opium and heroin had dropped significantly low. As a result, in a region overwhelmed with opium and heroin traffickers, the Taliban and their drug lords were not making large profits. By eliminating poppy production, but allowing opiate sales to continue, the Taliban and their drug smuggling compatriots were able to stock up on opium and heroin and sell it at significantly higher prices once others were no longer able to grow poppy. Considering most of this heroin goes to wealthy European nations, this action by the Taliban suddenly gave them an increasingly valuable commodity. Most likely, those drug lords with close relations to the Taliban were notified of the poppy ban before its occurrence, and were able to stockpile opiates, which sold it at very high prices. Meanwhile, the average poppy farmer lost out.

Large amounts of Afghani heroin are smuggled through regions of instability with Muslim ties. In recent years, heroin from the Golden Crescent was transferred to Europe via the "Balkan Route" of Turkey-Bulgaria-Macedonia-Albania and on to Italy and Greece,[100] where much of the heroin control in the region had transferred from Turkish to Albanian crime syndicates. Many of these Albanians have connections or are members of the Kosovo Liberation Army (KLA) terrorist organization. As a result, the KLA is able to purchase arms and finance their operations with revenues from the heroin trade. According to a U.S. Senate Republican Policy Committee report in March, 1999:

> The extensive Albanian crime network that extends throughout Europe and into North America, including allegations that a major portion of the KLA finances are derived from that network, mainly proceeds from drug trafficking; and

> Terrorist organizations motivated by the ideology of radical Islam, including assets of Iran and the notorious Osama Bin Laden—who has vowed a global terrorist war against Americans and American interests.[101]

Islamic extremist groups have ties with the heroin trade from Afghanistan to Europe, and even into North America. However, the Russian black market is also a large consumer of Afghan heroin, which brings in ties with the Russian Mafia, perhaps one of the most potentially dangerous and volatile liaisons in the world of terrorism today. Within the past two years, Southwest Asian heroin traffickers have found routes through the Central Asian countries of Uzbekistan, Kyrgyzstan, and Tajikistan, particularly via the Ferghana Valley, which is situated at the borders of all three countries.[102]

The danger in this Russian Mafia-Islamic Extremist relationship is that the Russian Mafia could be, or already is, providing Osama Bin Laden's Al Qaeda terrorist network with materials to produce weapons of mass destruction, such as chemical or radiological munitions.[103] Coincidentally, the Russian Mafia also has a strong hand in the trade of the drug commonly called "Ecstasy," which is popular in both the U.S. and Europe.

Of course, Central Asian terrorist/insurgent organizations and warlords also take advantage of the financial benefits of trafficking heroin through the region. One such group includes the Islamic Movement of Uzbekistan,[104] which was designated a terrorist organization by the U.S. State Department in late 2001.[105]

In the past, other Islamic extremist organizations may have had access to drug money. According to one source, Lebanon's Beka'a Valley was once belikened to Peru's Upper Huallaga Valley, with hashish instead of cocaine as a staple. The Beka'a Valley covers over 4200 square kilometers on Lebanon's eastern border with Syria, with Israel to the South. The hashish trade had been limited until Lebanon's civil war in 1975-1976. By the end of the war, with Lebanon heavily war-torn, various groups turned to trafficking hashish

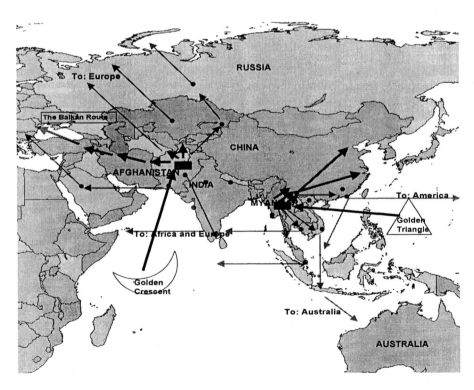

Asian Drug Flow
Information source: INTERPOL
Map made by Digital Mapping Center

to provide incomes. Even though Syria, whose profit from drug trafficking has been substantial, controlled most of the Beka'a Valley Palestinian terrorist groups also were able to join in the drug trade. The Palestine Liberation Organization (PLO), whose terrorist activities against United States citizens in the 1980s were well known, made millions of dollars from the trade.[106]

The Far East and the Golden Triangle

Numerous books have been written on the opium/heroin trade in the Golden Triangle, so this section will only touch on the subject. Terrorism, as defined in the first chapter, is not as well documented as a tactic in this region, but the wars in the Golden Triangle would at least fall under the definition of a *narco-insurgency*, or *drug-financed warfare*. In any event, this chapter would not be complete if the Golden Triangle region was never mentioned.

Opium has been a trade commodity in Southeast and East Asia for centuries. Although opium may have first appeared in the Far East as far back as 100 BC,[107] the opium *industry* began in the early 18th century when Britain began pushing opium into China at an ever-increasing rate.[108] By the early 19th century opium addiction infected China so badly that addicts were found among the king's court, and by 1832 even the military was partially debilitated. A sound defeat of the Chinese army by Yao rebels was partially attributed to the fact that "many of the troops from the coastal garrisons were opium smokers, and it was difficult to get any vigorous action from them."[109] Many troops from the same army deserted to search for opium.[110] In addition to the social harm, the opium problem caused virtually irrevocable damage to China's economy via the increasing outflow of silver, the currency of the opium trade. In 1793 China's silver reserve was estimated at 70 million taels of silver (approximately 2.6 million kilograms), but by 1820 this had been reduced to about 10 million taels.[111]

The situation became so dire that, in 1839, Lin Zexu (China's "Drug Czar") wrote his famous memorial to a young Queen Victoria, asking her: "Where is your conscience? I have heard that the smoking of opium is strictly forbidden by your country; this is because of the harm caused by opium is clearly understood. Since it is not permitted to do harm in your own country, then even less should you let it be passed on to the harm of other countries—how much less to China."[112] Britain's opium trafficking resulted in two "Opium Wars" with China, in 1839-1842, and 1856-1860, respectively. The first war resulted in China's eventual loss of Hong Kong as a British Crown Colony, and in the second China was forced to legalize the importation and sale of opium.[113] By 1900, one source estimated that China had as many as ninety million drug addicts.[114]

As mentioned earlier, Japan took advantage of China's opium problem for its own strategic gain. When communism took over China, opium use in the great nation was greatly decreased for a number of reasons, but opium in the Far East as a whole did not disappear. Just like every other example we have seen, the problem merely shifted locations.

The Golden Triangle, an area that straddles the tri-border area of Laos, Thailand, and Myanmar (Burma) just south of China, did not play a significant role in opium production in the time of the British opium trade. In fact, prior to World War II French and British colonialists led campaigns to halt opium production in this region in order to keep their revenues high, much as the Taliban recently did in Afghanistan.

But during the chaos of World War II and the communist takeover of China, the Golden Triangle was brought to the forefront of opium and heroin production. Many have implied that both the French colonialists and the Central Intelligence Agency (CIA) helped the poppy production increase from the 1940s through the 1960s, but for different reasons. While both were fighting against communism, French operatives needed opium to fund their operations—no different than many of the world's insurgencies.[115] The CIA, it seems, wanted alliance support as they covertly fought the spread of communism in the region. This support initially came from the Kuomintang, (KMT)—the former Nationalist Chinese who lost to the Communists—and the Hmong people in Laos. While the CIA did have its own funding, "by drawing on the resources of a powerful tribal leader or local warlord, a CIA agent could achieve a covert operational capacity far beyond his budgetary limits."[116]

The opiate trade in Laos existed long before the CIA ever entered the area. The French had monopolized the trade there, and were making a substantial profit from it. The KMT, which was also involved in the opium business in order to finance their army, probably had more than anyone to do with establishing the heroin domain of the Burmese section of the Golden Triangle. To blame the CIA for creating the Golden Triangle opium-growing region is probably not a fair statement. In fact, the CIA's workings with the KMT were more indirect. It was with the Hmong people, in Laos, that the CIA became implicated in the opiate trade. Perhaps author Martin Booth best explains why:

In order to check the spread of Communism in Asia, tribal headmen and warlords struck a deal with the French intelligence services and, more especially, with the CIA. By associating themselves with local leaders, CIA operatives were also building links with the opium business, for the two went hand in hand. Furthermore, to keep the warlords in power, the CIA allowed them to maintain their opium dealing and even provided them with open access to American munitions and air transport to further their opium or heroin distribution. In short, the CIA became inextricably entangled in the Golden Triangle....[117]

In all fairness, the CIA was in a lose-lose situation. The guys with the guns were the guys with the opium. With the mission to fight an effective covert war against communism in Southeast Asia, the CIA either had to allow their allies to continue to operate as before, or to supplement the local warring factions with arms and munitions. However, this latter action would have further complicated the issue by supplying U.S. arms to dangerous armies. Actions like this in the past have caused the U.S. intense problems. Recall the arming of Afghanistan soldiers with American Stingers during the Soviet-Afghan war—Stingers which popped up in other parts of the world after the war. Similarly, Saddam Hussein was provided with U.S arms to fight Iran prior to the Iraqi invasion of Kuwait.

The KMT's involvement in the opium and heroin trade set the stage for further narco-insurgency involvement. Other tribal leaders and local warlords controlled the various ethnic groups of the newly independent nation of Burma. Such groups, most of them located in the Golden Triangle region, included the Kachin Independent Army, the Kachin Liberation Army, the Lahu National Liberation Army, the United Wa State Army, the Shan State Army, the Shan National Army, the Shan National United Front, and the Shan United Army. To make the matter even more complex, these independent warring factions were fighting with the Burmese government—whom the U.S. was not at war with—for independence. Since the Golden Triangle was a no-man's-land, with few roads in or out of the area, opium became the only commodity these factions could survive on. General Tuan Shi-wen, a veteran of the covert wars in Burma, stated quite bluntly: "To fight you must have an army, and an army must have guns, and to buy guns you must have money. In these mountains the only money is opium."[118]

Probably the most famous of the Golden Triangle warlords was Khun Sa, leader of the Shan United Army (which later joined with other groups to form the Mong Tai Army, also under Khun Sa's leadership) who had proclaimed himself "King of the Golden Triangle." Khun Sa took this stand on his dealings in opium: "I know it is a social evil and understand the damage it does, not only to the West, but among my own people. But I do not feel guilty. What we are doing is justified."[119] His people needed the arms to fight their war.

During the 1960s, about the same time Khun Sa was gaining a monopoly on the heroin trade in the Golden Triangle, the highly secretive but very powerful Chinese crime organizations—the Triads—began to internationalize heroin trafficking from the guerrilla-controlled "Golden Triangle."[120] This heroin was pushed onto American soldiers in Vietnam, and as a result the Triads eventually were able to traffic their product for use inside the United States.

In 1996, Khun Sa and the Mong Tai Army surrendered to the Burmese government, and today organizations such as the United Wa State Army (USWA) and the Myanmar National Democratic Alliance Army (Kokang Chinese) have a strong grip on the opium trade of the Golden Triangle. While Mexican and Colombian heroin currently make up the majority of the American market, heroin from the Golden Triangle is still to be found on American streets. The USWA is also Asia's largest methamphetamine supplier. This drug has blazed its way into Thailand.

The Golden Triangle is probably as complex as any of the major drug producing areas, and it is not likely to go away soon. With China's entry into the World Trade Organization, opiate and methamphetamines traffickers will have many of the same benefits and opportunities that Latin American drug traffickers obtained with NAFTA.

America and Its Borders

Within the past several years, violence and terrorism associated with Mexican drug trafficking (cocaine, marijuana, and heroin) has become so horrendous that President Bill Clinton predicted that Mexicans "will, in the end, not be able to maintain the fabric of an orderly, democratic and free society if the narco-traffickers come to dominate huge sections of their country." This violence was well portrayed in the hit movie *Traffic*.

Recently, the Mexican drug violence problem has spread into the United States. In the summer of 1996, a rancher from the southwestern United States (wearing a hood to hide his identity) testified before a Senate committee that he had to flee his ranch, owned for two generations, due to drug violence. He stated that heavily-armed drug dealers from Mexico terrorized his family in broad daylight. Other ranchers refused to testify for fear of retaliation.[121]

Over the past decade severe crime and violence has also grown in our own American streets and neighborhoods, due in considerable part to the vast expansion of street gangs. While gang violence only borders on the "formal" definition of terrorism, it merits comment.

Despite major efforts by police and other law enforcement agencies to reduce violence in American neighborhoods, gangs have much control; they "own" entire regions of major cities. This territorial expansion is referred to as "Gang Imperialism,"[122] and drugs are becoming the same economic force for gangs today as alcohol was during Prohibition. A mid-level member of a well-reputed American gang and drug distributor for the organization over a four-state region estimates that approximately 80 percent of the financial support for her gang comes from illegal drug sales.[123]

Once a gang has defined its territory, its next step is to defend it from outsiders. Gangs defend their "turf" in order to protect their particular business, and illegal drugs are a major part of that business. Each street corner, dope house, dealer, distributor, or customer is part of that territory. Anyone attempting to enter the area becomes the invader, the intruder, and the enemy. However, unlike the legitimate business world, gangs use physical violence as their only enforcement tool to stop competition and opposition.[124]

In September 1995, four-year-old Stephanie Kuhen was shot and killed by hoodlums when her mother's boyfriend made a wrong turn into a dead-end street in Los Angeles, California. The gangs had marked the "turf" as "Avenue of Killers." The gang barricaded the car with trashcans, and then opened fire. Stephanie was hit in the head as she lay in her mother's arms. One local couple blamed drug dealers as the real problem. Indications are that the local gang used the territory for drug sales.[125]

In September 1995, a teen-aged assassin shot an anti-gang prosecutor in the face, a tactic common among Colombian terrorists. American drug users are creating an outlaw culture employed by the narcotics industry—an industry generating substantial money and, therefore, substantial power. This power has allowed gangs to become the massive institutions of violence they have developed into. It also allows them to become mobile, and this mobility leads to the expansion of territorial boundaries well beyond the few blocks of their respective neighborhoods. Illegal drug revenues have also given gangs high-tech equipment with which to operate. Such equipment includes Night Vision Goggles, communications encryption devices, boats, aircraft, radar, electronic surveillance equipment (which aided one gang in tracking down and killing a police-protected witness by listening to police radio traffic) and automatic weapons.

In parts of eastern Kentucky, where much of the U.S.-grown marijuana is cultivated, one source described the situation as almost Colombia-like. "Growers and traffickers [of marijuana] have disrupted the tranquility of the communities and public lands." It went on to state that:

> Crime and corruption of public officials are directly linked to the marijuana trade, creating fear among the citizens. Local economies and political institutions are adversely affected [by the marijuana trade], thus, creating a more totalitarian and oppressive environment for the populace of some local communities.[126]

In Puerto Rico, a United States Commonwealth, Puerto Rican superintendent Pedro Toledo stated that 80 percent of the murders in 1996 in his country were directly related to drug trafficking, while another 10 percent were indirectly attributed to drug trafficking.[127] Such violence prompted one Puerto Rican citizen to explain, "I don't think Washington has done enough for us. It is only concerned about stopping drugs from getting to the mainland. Meanwhile, we are getting killed out here."[128]

Summary

Manifestations of narco-terrorism are seemingly endless. Surprisingly, considering its long history, narco-terrorism has received very little attention. Yet many Americans, through their drug habits, are not only financing violent destruction in war-torn countries such as Colombia, but in their own country also.

The impact of the financial support of common drug users on violent organizations is significant. History has shown that more armies have been ruined by the inability to supply themselves than by enemy forces.[129] Drug money enables violent organizations around the world to provide themselves with supplies. Even though terrorist organizations such as the Shining Path come and go, the drug money is always there to finance the next violent, terrorist organization.

Chapter 3
Historical Efforts to Fight the Drug War

Initially, unaware (or unconcerned) with the narco-terrorist/insurgent relationship, the countries of the Western Hemisphere fought narco-trafficking as a solitary problem, and chose methods that were generally ineffective. While Latin American states approached the drug problem unilaterally, the United States sought to encourage bilateral cooperation, but often with a unilateral "my way or the highway" approach. American authorities tried to focus on the problem through interdiction and eradication, but the drug-producing states saw the real source of the problem as demand in the United States. As narco-trafficking and drug addiction rose throughout the Americas, Latin American states began to explore the idea of using concerted international action to fight the drug problem.[1]

Former Peruvian President Alan Garcia described Transnational Drug "Cartels" (TDCs) as Latin America's first successful multinational corporations.[2] The international scope of the drug problem eventually came to the attention of Latin American countries through the Organization of American States (OAS). By the early 1980s, the OAS had perceived illegal drug activity as a hemispheric security threat. A summit meeting in August 1984 attended by delegates from Bolivia, Colombia, Venezuela and Ecuador produced the *Declaration of Quito* which pronounced drug-trafficking a crime against mankind, and the OAS took up the issue at its 14th General Assembly later that year. The OAS concurred with the declaration and convened the Inter-American Specialized Conference on "Traffic of Narcotic Drugs" in Rio de Janeiro in April 1986. Participants at the conference declared that drug trafficking jeopardized the values of human rights, democracy, the environment, and national sovereignty. The delegates passed two significant resolutions. First, they established guidelines that each state could use in its own effort to combat the drug problem. Second, they brought the OAS, an international organization, into the drug war.[3]

The primary objectives of the Program of Action adopted at the Rio Conference were to "reduce the demand for drugs, prevent drug abuse, and effectively combat unlawful production of and trafficking in drugs."[4] However, even though the Program of Action represented an inter-American agreement on how to fight the drug problem, it provided only *guidelines* for individual member states, not *requirements*, and individual countries could not be held accountable for their action or inaction. Two years later, in Guatemala City, another OAS gathering proclaimed the American Alliance Against Drug Trafficking. This declaration underscored the need for collective action to counter transnational drug trafficking operations. The Guatemala Conference also created the Inter-American Drug Abuse Control Commission (CICAD), the first international effort to fight the war on drugs in the Western Hemisphere. Complete with its own Secretary General, CICAD is a non-enforcement agency designed to develop, coordinate, and monitor the program of collective action. CICAD concerns itself primarily with five areas of action:[5]

1) development of a legal framework (harmonizing national narcotics laws and improving law enforcement cooperation);
2) education for prevention of drug abuse;
3) community mobilization;
4) maintenance of the Inter-American Data Bank and Uniform Drug Statistical System;
5) maintenance of the Inter-American Drug Documentation and Information Center and the Inter-American Drug Information System.

Concepts for the use of force to fight the drug problem had surfaced, but had not received support.

The much-needed effort to fight the powerful drug cartels with transnational cooperation had finally materialized, and the efforts of CICAD and the declaration of Guatemala continue today. The Santiago Commitment to Democracy and the Renewal of the Inter-American System (Santiago Commitment), another cooperative pact adopted June 4, 1991, encouraged the following:

... the adoption and execution of appropriate measures to prevent and combat the illicit use and production of narcotic drugs and psychotropic substances, and traffic therein, chemical precursors and money laundering, and related clandestine traffic in arms, ammunition, and explosives.[6]

In May of 1998, CICAD produced a comprehensive anti-drug strategy and an "Action Plan" to implement it. The strategy stressed an international unity of effort to reduce demand and supply, and the adoption of control measures such as dismantling of criminal organizations. The Action Plan best sums up the strategy presented:

1) assist with institutional strengthening in member states to promote collaboration (integration) among agencies, ministries and other entities responsible for the various aspects of the country's response to the drug problem;
2) assist with training (relates to all priority lines of action and programs of CICAD);
3) assist countries in data base development and data gathering regarding all aspects of the drug issue;
4) assist countries with the identification of sources of money to support implementation of the strategy;
5) develop impact indicators regarding programs and initiatives; and
6) identify and compile information concerning existing training activities being carried out by agencies/organizations and further coordinate training initiatives being contemplated by CICAD with these existing programs.[7]

But while the OAS stresses international cooperation, two prevailing circumstances ensure the continuing dominance of unilateral measures. First, although international cooperation is growing, it is still a slow process. In the meantime, transnational drug cartels cross international borders at will, and national counterdrug forces must stop them at the border. Rarely is the nation on the other side of the border ready to assume authority. For example, a Peruvian air force jet may be chasing a drug trafficking aircraft and ready to force a landing. When the trafficker flies across the border into Brazil's Amazon "no-man's-land," the Peruvians must give up the chase.

The second circumstance arises from a unilateral strategy developed in the mid-1980s by the United States to ensure that each country in the drug war would be held accountable for doing its part. In the belief that some drug-producing states were making an insufficient effort to rid their nations of illegal drugs, the United States Congress added an amendment to its 1961 Foreign Assistance Act, mandating "certification." The Foreign Assistance Act had begun as a means of providing aid to foreign states as a further deterrent to Soviet aggression during the Cold War. However, the 1986 amendment authorized the United States to create a certification system of aid leveraging, that is, to "de-certify," or suspend aid to drug-producing nations which were perceived to be uncooperative in the war on drugs.[8]

To assist in this certification process the United States developed a list of major drug-producing and drug-transit countries. A major drug-producing country is defined as one where at least 1,000 hectares of opium poppy or coca, or 5,000 hectares of cannabis are cultivated or harvested per year, unless the President of the United States determines that such illicit cannabis production does not significantly affect the United States.[9] A major drug-transit country is defined as one that is either a significant direct source of illicit narcotic or psychotropic drugs affecting the United States, or one through which drugs are transported.[10]

If a country is on the "majors" list, the United States President must "certify" its government as cooperating satisfactorily to combat drug-trafficking before aid can be provided. If certification is denied, aid that can be withheld includes arms, food assistance, and loans, leaving only specified humanitarian and counter-narcotics assistance.

The United States can also execute a "vital national interests certification." In such a case American vital interests require that assistance not be withheld, even though a country does not meet the requirements of full certification. A country that receives vital national interest certification is eligible for the same aid as a fully certified one.[11] While the intent sounds appropriate, serious problems can occur, as we shall see later in this chapter.

On 11 January, 2000, Washington undertook a major bilateral approach to aiding Colombia in its efforts to solve its huge trafficking problem. President Clinton announced a 2-year, $1.6 billion assistance package to support Colombian President Pastrana's plan to achieve peace, fight crime, promote prosperity, and improve government (the plan outlay eventually came to $1.313 billion).[12] The "Colombian Plan" has five components: 1) Improving Governing Capacity and Respect for Human Rights, 2) Expansion of Counter-Narcotics Operations Into Southern Colombia, 3) Alternative Economic Development, 4) Increased Interdiction in Colombia and the Region, and 5) Assistance for the Colombian National Police.[13] This plan is vitally important to Colombia, and may have rescued it from an unsalvageable situation. The plan also supports programs which will attempt to prevent coca cultivation from spreading or retreating back into Peru and Bolivia.

The Colombia Plan has both supporters and critics. Ambassador David Passage, former director of Andean Affairs in the Latin American Bureau of the United States Department of State, is among the critics. Passage chastises the Colombian government for misapplication of resources (trying to obtain high-tech equipment it does not need to fight guerrillas), and Washington for using the Vietnam syndrome as an excuse not to get more involved in this guerrilla war.[14] Others show that the plan is already meeting with success. It is still too early, however, to predict its long-term effects.

Despite all the efforts described above, illegal drug activity still thrives. For this I find six main reasons, each of which will be discussed in the remainder of this chapter: 1) no assurance of international cooperation for any counter-narcotics plan; 2) the OAS Charter provision denying foreign armies the right to cross international borders to pursue narco-traffickers; 3) inefficiencies of the Certification system; 4) public ignorance in the United States of narco-terrorism, and Washington's refusal to fight narco-trafficking and guerrilla insurgencies as a single entity (although since 9/11 the new Bush administration clearly sees the two problems as inter-connected); 5) the United States methodology used to fight the drug war; and 6), the United States' inability to stop drug consumption.

1) Although CICAD bases its strategy on a unity of effort, there is no mechanism to ensure the cooperation of each country. There is no way of verifying whether or not a member country is complying with specified CICAD recommendations. For example, a country may choose not to collaborate with other countries (by sharing intelligence or information) that might cast the first country's anti-drug effort in a negative light. Moreover, many Latin American countries do not experience internal problems from drug production, and therefore commit their resources, assets, and training to problems deemed more important than those considered in the Action Plan. Colombia did not seem interested in stopping the flow of cocaine to the United States until the FARC and ELN began to build a threatening presence with drug money. It was only when Colombia finally became aware of the magnitude of the narco-terrorist issue that the government realized it did not have the police or military forces to fight the problem.

Brazil was also slow to develop an interest in the drug trafficking activity that had developed on its jungle borders. This was seen during the "air bridge" campaign in Peru in the early 1990s. Instances of Peruvian air force jets chasing drug traffickers up to the Brazilian border as described above often occurred. Once across the border, the traffickers could proceed through Brazil unpursued. The Colombian cartels have taken advantage of Brazil in another way also: they use Amazon tribes to transport illegal drugs to Colombia for processing. As a result of Brazil's noninvolvement, both drug trafficking and drug use increased significantly in Brazil, and the government has now been compelled to establish, amongst other things, an Amazon Surveillance System at the cost of $1.4 billion to help track illegal drug traffickers.[15]

It is also true that individual strategies of different countries may not be agreeable to other nations. A clear example of this came when Peruvian President Fujimori disagreed with United States method of fighting the drug war to such a degree that he rejected aid to make his point.

2) CICAD, in compliance with the OAS founding principles, must respect the sovereignty and territorial integrity of countries. That is, Latin American militaries will not step on the soil of a neighboring country. While this is a sound principle, in this case it results in an international mechanism (drug trafficking) being attacked by a multitude of smaller, border-locked, separate entities with different goals, different motivations, and different resources. Each country's strategy may not be in concert with others, and drug traffickers can use different laws and borders to work to their advantage. While militaries may work unilaterally (or at best bilaterally) in the drug war, the drug lords are working multi-nationally, with no concept of borders.

3) The United States unilateral certification effort does not have its intended effect. The idea of certification, of course, is to promote cooperation in the drug war, even if forced, but more often than not the outcome has been conflict. Since its inception, the certification process has come under criticism from the international community, and today it has domestic opponents as well. Peter Hakim, President of Inter-American Dialogue, claims that certification "often isolates and weakens our potentially most reliable partner (in the fight against drugs and other areas as well) and bolsters those who resist cooperation."[16] Former U.S. Representative Lee H. Hamilton (D-Ind) has stated that certification "does not lead to increased cooperation in the international fight against narcotics. In fact, it discourages it."[17] While some countries angrily view de-certification as a slap in the face in front of the international community, other decertified countries, such as Myanmar and Afghanistan, are clearly unconcerned about their de-certified status.

Certification has resulted in additional criticism because it is inevitably a political process that results in differential treatment. Mexico and Colombia are cases in point. Nearly two-thirds of all American-bound drugs enter the U.S. through Mexico. DEA sources state that Mexican drug traffickers are taking over most of the Baja and Yucatan peninsulas, as well as most of the areas west and south of Mexico City. One result is the heavy flow of the low-priced, "black tar" heroin, "which can mean rapid addiction or, if overdosed, a quick death for American Youths."[18] Black tar heroin, known as *chiva* in Mexico, was the drug that caused the "Texas Heroin Massacre," in which eighteen teens died in three years and over 75 were hospitalized near death in one year in the small, wealthy Dallas suburb of Plano.[19] Mexican traffickers also have a monopoly on methamphetamine trafficking in the United States.[20]

Senior Mexican authorities are taking the drug threat very seriously. According to the United States State Department, Mexico has used up to 20,000 military soldiers daily in drug eradication efforts,[21] and Mexico's 2000 counter-drug budget was $1 billion, a price which has a higher per capita percentage than Washington spends fighting its drug war.[22]

Mexico's National Program for the Control of Drugs 1995-2000 was an aggressive plan which has fostered United States-Mexican joint efforts. In 1995 Mexico and the U.S. signed the Financial Information Exchange Agreement to fight money laundering between the two nations, and in 1998 they agreed on the Bi-National Drug Strategy and its accompanying Performance Measures Effectiveness treaties, which provide guidelines for mutual goals in combating drug trafficking and organized crime.[23] According to Pentagon officials the two countries share effective bilateral military-to-military cooperation,[24] and joint US-Mexican efforts include the provisions of equipment and training by both law enforcement and military to their Mexican counterparts in the fight against drug trafficking.

However, joint United States-Mexican counter-narcotics cooperation, as well as unilateral efforts by the Mexican government are seriously hampered by corruption in Mexico. Former DEA chief Thomas Constantine recently called the attention of a Senate narcotics control caucus to the "unparalleled corruption within Mexican law enforcement agencies."[25] Even Mexico's own counter-narcotics chief was arrested on charges of being on the payroll of Mexico's most powerful drug lords in 1997.

This infamous corruption in Mexico, as explained in Chapter One, makes American officials wary of sharing sensitive information with their Mexican counterparts. According to the *Christian Science Monitor*:

> A number of high-level investigators with an elite, US-trained unit failed to pass required lie detector tests when asked about contacts with drug dealers. US officials worry intelligence they've passed to the unit went straight to traffickers.[26]

Judd Gregg, Chairman of the Senate Appropriations Committee on Commerce, Justice, State and Judiciary, plainly said:

> Corruption continues to pervade the law enforcement commu-

nity to the point where the DEA has serious reservations about even dealing with the law enforcement community of Mexico.[27]

When, in 1998, American agents launched a sting operation in Mexico which became the "largest, most comprehensive drug money laundering case in the history of U.S. law enforcement," American officials were not able to alert Mexican authorities to the operation for fear of information leaks. In fact, American law enforcement officials even told Mexican authorities before the operation that none of their undercover work would take place on Mexican soil.[28]

Such covert efforts by the United States are required to offset Mexican failures in countering drug trafficking. Thomas Constantine declared:

> Because there is little effective law enforcement activity leading to arrest of major traffickers in Mexico, U.S. law enforcement must be...more aggressive in identifying, targeting and arresting the highest level drug traffickers who are working in the U.S. at the behest of Mexican drug lords.[29]

Perhaps Senator Charles Grassley (R-Iowa), chairman of the Senate Caucus on International Narcotics Control, may have said it best when he stated: "Mexico may be doing all it can. If so, we have a lot to be concerned about, because it isn't enough."[30]

As a result of this corruption, Mexico has not performed any better than narco-paralyzed Colombia. Yet, in 1998 Mexico received full certification from Washington, while Colombia was decertified. Colombia is a smaller country (only 38 million people), geographically and economically unimportant to the United States, and Washington is perhaps less reluctant to use economic pressure to gain its objectives.[31] Decertifying Mexico, on the other hand, could have grave economic repercussions. A strong Mexican economy is necessary for the United States, since the two countries share a 2,000-mile border and both are members of the North American Free Trade Agreement (NAFTA). To cut off aid to a neighbor that has a population of 95 million, and which is one of America's most important trading partners, would have a severe negative impact on the American economy. In addition, such an initiative would probably cause even greater illegal immigration into the United States when the Mexican economy faltered as a result.

Despite Mexico's spotty record in anti-drug cooperation, the United States provided an emergency $50 billion bailout package during Mexico's peso devaluation crisis in December 1994. Post-communist Russia, the state of Israel, and Europe during the Marshall Plan were never given such aid in a single payment. Obviously, cutting aid via decertification is not an option for the U.S. vis-à-vis Mexico. Yet if this is the case, why choose full certification rather than "vital national interests" certification, other than to save political embarrassment for our NAFTA neighbor? Which then raises the question: why have certification at all? The United States congress is at least asking this question, and Senators Barbara Boxer (D-Cal) and Phil Gramm (R-Texas) led an effort to revamp the entire certification process.[32]

President Clinton certified both Mexico and Colombia for 1999 and 2000, when Drug Czar Barry McCaffrey praised Mexico for its battle against drugs. McCaffrey's remarks coincided with DEA chief Constantine's harsh criticism of Mexico and his abrupt retirement. Interestingly, U.S. Representatives John Mica (R-Florida), chairman of the subcommittee that handles drug policy, and Benjamin Gilman (R-NY), chairman of the International Relations committee, attempted to withdraw the certification of Mexico in 2000, but without success.

Washington's attitude toward Colombia, on the other hand, has been much more rigid. In 1998 Washington decertified Colombia in part because of controversial evidence that the Colombian president at the time, Ernesto Samper, had accepted drug money for his presidential election. However, Samper did not seem a likely candidate for cooperation with the drug cartels. He was openly anti-drug, and the cartels were behind an assassination attempt on Samper in 1989 that nearly killed him. Samper maintained his hardline against narco-traffickers. He put seven Cali Cartel drug lords in jail and eradicated more illicit opium poppies and coca plants than any administration in history.[33] Meanwhile, he asked the world not to "demonize" Colombia, saying his country was more of a victim than a villain in the drug war, and he approached the United Nations with a five-point plan against "narco-terrorism."[34] He also took a bold anti-drug stance by encouraging legislation to revoke the constitutional ban on the extradition of Colombian drug lords to the United States.[35] Colombia had outlawed extradition in 1991 during a deadly campaign of bombings, assassinations, and kidnappings by the drug lords, including the M19 attack on the Palace of Justice. To assassinate such an active anti-drug president would have brought too much world attention to the narco-terrorism reality. Destroying his reputation was a much more effective, *indirect* approach.

Adding to the controversy surrounding Samper was the discovery of eight pounds of heroin on his plane prior to his departure to the United

Nations Assembly.[36] The Colombian government called the incident a setup by drug lords to embarrass Samper and further degrade his reputation, and most likely this is true. The very idea that a country's president, one whom the drug lords had tried to assassinate, who was already under allegations of accepting drug money for his campaign, and whose country Washington had decertified, would attempt to fly illegal drugs into the United States is nothing short of ludicrous.

To some observers, the American government in this situation was acting hypocritically. After all, while Samper was being accused of accepting donations from drug lords, Vice-President Albert Gore accepted $20,000 from, and invited to the White House, drug trafficker Jorge Cabrera.[37] And while it is true that Colombia provides the largest percentage of the world's cocaine, it is also true that the United States provides the most consumers of their illicit drugs. As Samper fought a war against the narco-terrorists who paralyzed his country and nearly killed him, President Clinton laughingly confessed in front of the nation's youth on MTV that, if given another chance, he would inhale marijuana.[38] Clinton later pardoned several criminals convicted for drug trafficking.

The certification process can provide some leverage to fight the drug war, and in March of 2001 President George W. Bush decertified both Afghanistan and Myanmar for their obvious lack of effort in the drug war. However, the past decertifications of Colombia by the world's largest consumer of drugs seemed to make the process a system to create scapegoats, rather than promote cooperation. The division caused by the certification process in a hemisphere trying to achieve unity in the drug war undermines efforts to combat a problem that requires both multinational and domestic support. President Bush, whose recently held office as the Texas Governor, has a strong knowledge of the issues surrounding Mexico and many other Latin American nations, rightly certified both Mexico and Colombia.

4) Washington has not sufficiently addressed the issue of narco-terrorism (this has been slowly changing after 9/11). As early as 1987 terrorist experts, such as John Thackrah, argued that an alliance between narco-traffickers and terrorists/insurgents existed and that it is wrong "to treat the drug issue and terrorism problem on separate agendas."[39] Peru achieved considerable success in the drug war, especially with its crop substitution programs, *after* the defeat of the Shining Path.

Even more recently, Bolivia eliminated an emerging narco-terrorism threat in its country from the very start, before it could get out of control. Bolivia was once the second largest producer of coca (behind one-time leader

Peru). The Bolivian government relied solely on crop substitution efforts to decrease coca cultivation, but the coca growers did not find the financial benefits worth the effort, and resisted government substitution efforts. The Bolivian government then phased out voluntary eradication and turned to forced eradication, using the military and police. That decision first provoked protests by coca growers and then, in the wake of a government crackdown, it led to the formation of "self-defense committees" by peasants who conducted ambushes and raids on army and police units. Fearing a guerrilla "narco-terrorist" insurrection, the government brought the Anti-Terrorism National Center into the drug fight. Within months the rebellion collapsed, and so has the lucrative illegal drug business in Bolivia.[40] "I don't have to like it," one Bolivian coca farmer commented, "but coca has no future."[41] Former Bolivian President, Hugo Banzar, believes that the illegal crop may be completely eradicated by the year 2002.

Any attempt to stop and replace cocaine and heroin production in areas under heavy FARC and ELN guardianship simply will not work without a strategy and force capable of eliminating the rebels. However, Washington demands that Colombia not use American provided counter-drug aid in the effort to fight the guerrillas. Colombia, therefore, is forced to fight the war against narco-terrorism on separate fronts. Yet the experiences of Peru and Bolivia indicate that success in combating narco-trafficking cannot be assured unless narco-terrorism as a whole is attacked.

5) The methodology that has been used to fight the drug war is a failure. Law Enforcement Agencies (LEAs) are being forced to fight this narco-terrorism issue with limited (and sometimes no) military support. The United States does provide indirect military support to its LEAs, but the drug war may require more than that (at least outside American borders). To see the problem clearly, one needs to understand the drug war itself. This, in turn, requires knowledge of Low Intensity Conflicts (LIC), a technical subject that encompasses insurgent/guerrilla warfare.

Transnational drug operations can be likened to an insurgency, as drug smuggling operations resemble (and use tactics comparable to) insurgent warfare. An insurgency is normally divided into three elements. First, there is the underground organization. This is the covert "headquarters" of the element, or in the case of the narcotics trade, drug lords (whether they be high ranking drug traffickers or guerrilla leaders). It normally possesses a cellular structure to protect the rest of the system from being incapacitated should one of the cells be compromised.

The auxiliary is the second element. It works to support the narco-traffickers but does not actively participate in the trafficking itself. It provides couriers, equipment (such as processing chemicals), and transportation (other than moving the merchandise itself); however, most importantly, it provides information. It acts as eyes and ears for the narco-traffickers and drug lords. Auxiliary personnel are often "common citizens," who conduct their activities secretly.

Finally, there is the "guerrilla force," or the actual producers and traffickers. They are the action side that actually produce and move the drugs; however, unlike an actual guerrilla force, the producers and traffickers quite often cannot provide their own security. Therefore, the "headquarters" will usually hire guerrilla forces or terrorist units as security, or have the guerrillas conduct drug production and local transportation operations themselves—thus creating the "narco-terrorism" link.

Additionally, as narco-terrorism is a double-edged sword, the drug traffickers play a reverse role and act as an auxiliary to the insurgents in Latin American countries by providing funds and logistical support, often transporting weapons from other countries.

Quite simply, narco-trafficking looks like and acts like an insurgency. Normally, military forces are used to fight against guerrilla forces. Certainly no police force was ever going to fight the Taliban—who fought a heroin-financed insurgency to gain power. But in the drug war most militaries have been given only limited authority to participate, or are too weak to fight the drug problem even if the co-existing terrorist-insurgent problem did not exist. Yet, with memories such as the Vietnam War and Soviet operations in Afghanistan still lingering so recently in our world's history, no one wants to exert too much force—like committing military units—into another guerrilla-type conflict. The idea of using military force, especially in Latin America, also brings legitimate fears of totalitarianism and human rights abuses. Legitimacy for direct military force is not accepted by many nations, particularly for the superpower that provides the logistical and financial support—the United States. For these reasons the drug war is fought with weak militaries that do not have U.S. support, or police-style counter-narcotics forces, rather than with a professional force large enough and strong enough to handle the problem.

6) Even if the international community used the military to fight the drug war, too many drug users are still willing to buy the drugs, and the welfare of too many peasant farmers depends on growing illegal drug-producing plants. Traffickers will still take risks to make millions of dollars as

long as they have people to buy the drugs and people to grow them. It is crucial that drug demand must be lowered, and viable crop substitution for illegal drugs must be available.

The next chapter further examines these problems, and prescribes a strategy to overcome the built-in dilemmas and accomplish the double end of winning the war on drugs and eliminating narco-terrorism. The strategy presented has four phases. Each phase is a continuous process, proceeding as a "Unified Strategy." These phases are education, extradition, a specialized inter-regional paramilitary force, and civic action through eradication and crop substitution.

Chapter 4

A Unified Strategy

Narco-terrorism is an extraordinary type of conflict the nature of which much of the world has not wholly grasped. Whereas trafficking in illegal drugs is considered a crime, terrorism is a political weapon short of war, and insurgencies are a type of warfare; narco-terrorism involves all three. Max G. Manwaring has characterized such complex issues as Gray Area Phenomena (GAPs).[1] He describes GAP conflicts as "threats to the stability of nation states by non-state actors and non-governmental processes and organizations," which involve "immense regions or urban areas where control has shifted from legitimate governments to new half political, half criminal powers."[2] Manwaring cites insurgencies, terrorism, drug trafficking, and narco-terrorism among examples of GAPs.

Manwaring identifies and examines sixty-nine GAP-type conflicts that have occurred since World War II and develops a paradigm by which one can effectively tackle these conflict situations. The "Manwaring Paradigm" states that the outcome of a GAP will be determined by the following factors:[3]

1) the strength and weakness of a country's governmental institutions, i.e., the degree of a regime's legitimacy;
2) the ability to reduce outside support for an illegal challenger;
3) the type and consistency of outside support for the targeted government;
4) the credibility of objectives and degree of organization for unity of effort;
5) the level of discipline and capabilities of the security forces; and
6) the effectiveness of the intelligence apparatus.

If these variables favor the incumbent government, it has a greater chance of winning the conflict. Manwaring does not describe the specific methods by which a GAP conflict can be won, as each GAP scenario is situation-dependent. Rather, he provides a textbook-like solution for GAPs, much like the type of army field manual used by an infantry company commander to implement an offensive attack. As this chapter examines the phases of a sound strategy to defeat narco-terrorism, it takes into account each of the six Manwaring variables.

The four phases of the *Unified Strategy* include education on narco-terrorism, extradition, a specialized force, and civic action. The first two phases deal primarily with inhibiting the appetite in the United States for drugs from foreign sources (they will not necessarily deter drugs produced domestically), thereby curtailing the flow of money from U.S. drug users to terrorist organizations. In the last two phases, conducted in the international arena itself, the U.S. would probably need to lead or assist in some of the efforts. The first two phases are intended to significantly reduce the financial support of drug revenues to terrorists and insurgents; the last two phases are required to deal the final blow to narco-terrorism.

Phase I. Education on Narco-Terrorism

Demand is the most significant factor in the drug war. Simply put: "Without the rich, pleasure-seeking U.S. consumer culture, the [drug] trade would be insignifi-cant."[4]   President George W. Bush clearly identified the significance of the demand issue when he stated during John Walters' nomination as Director of the Executive Office of the National Drug Control Policy (ONDCP): "the most effective way to reduce the supply of drugs in America is to reduce the demand for drugs in America."

Because of this, eliminating demand should be the *center of gravity* for a strategy in the drug war. Military theorists define the center of gravity as "those vital areas that if damaged or destroyed will unbalance the enemy's entire structure," resulting in the complete failure of the enemy's effort.[5] Classic military theorist Carl Von Clausewitz defined this idea as the "hub of all power and movement, on which everything depends."

As the strategic center of gravity, the elimination of demand becomes the "main effort" (as a military staff would refer to it) in combating narco-terrorism. As I once heard Lieutenant Colonel John Caruthers of Fort Benning's Infantry schoolhouse once describe the main effort: "If we do *this*, we win." One fact of the drug war is certain, if America stops using drugs, the traffickers will have to look elsewhere for a market, and "we win." For that reason, all other efforts should be considered supporting efforts to the main effort of eliminating demand. Perhaps Lieutenant Colonel Earl Bell of the National Guard Bureau-Counterdrug Office provided the best example of victory in this drug war when I heard him state: "If we could get 10 out of 10 kids who, upon seeing a truck load of Ecstasy dumped in the driveway, would pick up shovels and put the stuff in the trash, we've won."

But one should never forget that the main effort and all supporting efforts of any strategy must work in harmony with one another. If not, the "enemy" can slip away and live to fight another day, or can focus all its forces against the main effort and possibly steal the victory.

As mentioned earlier, the "drug war" in and of itself can be likened to countering an insurgency, or Low Intensity Conflict (LIC), as narco-traffickers use the same principles to conduct their operations as guerrilla leaders use to guide an insurgency. According to the Department of the Army *Field Manual 100-20. Military Operations in Low Intensity Conflict,* a LIC is a "confrontation between contending groups below conventional war"[6] involving competing principles while threatening the stability of established nations by use of political, military, economic, and *informational* means. Insurgencies are rarely defeated solely on the battlefield; rather, they are won or lost in the arenas of political action (or inaction) and popular support. During the Tet Offensive in the Vietnam War, for example, the U.S. military won the battles, but the North Vietnamese won the political battle as American popular support for the war wavered.[7] The *Information War* can heavily influence the playing field of the drug war, and education is the tool.

According to former President George Bush's National Drug Control Strategy (NDCS) of 1992, "one of the most important goals of the NDCS is to prevent Americans, especially the young, from ever using drugs."[8] [9] He was right, and the United States (one of the world's primary users of illegal drug)[10] has used education as an important tactic in its strategy to combat drug use.

Yet past drug education programs did not seem to have the desired effect, particularly with the primary target group, the nation's youth. As President Clinton aptly noted in 1995: "Simplistic prevention messages of the past appear not to work for today's young people."[11] Drug use rose steadily from 1993 to the late 1990s. Although in 1999 drug education efforts caused a slight decline in drug use among the 12 to 17 year-old age group, drug use among the 18 to 25 year-old age group continued to increased.[12] Similarly, trends increased for emergency room problems related to cocaine, heroin, methamphetamines, and marijuana use. Perhaps this is because education about the ill effects that drugs can have on their physical and mental health is not yet important to many teenagers. It is worth asking why this might be so.

First, physically, a teenage body suffering from moderate drug abuse is still more likely to perform better than the average adult body. Moreover, teenagers often feel a sense of "invincibility" when it comes to their physical health and well-being. A case in point is the failure of the anti-smoking campaigns of the past decade. Despite some short-term reduction in teenage smoking during the peek of the campaigns (which included such tactics as showing teen "superstar" Brooke Shields with cigarettes sticking out of her nose and ears), and the well-known health hazards of smoking, teen smoking rates are as high today as they were in the 1970s.[13] In fact, an effort in Canada to get teens to stop smoking by including graphic pictures in warning labels on cigarette packs left many teens unmoved. The pictures, which showed photos of smoking-related health hazards such as tooth decay and rotting lungs, had no effect. "They scare me a bit," said one seventh grade girl who had been smoking for a year, "but it doesn't stop me from smoking. I like it too much."[14] At least one store employee selling cigarettes testified that "young people find them [the graphic adds] funny. They're so gross that they're laughing at them."[15]

This sense of immortality, or lack of self-concern by people in their teens (and early 20s), is acknowledged as a clinical condition called the "high-risk behavior syndrome." Dr. Dennis R. Sparkman, former faculty member at the University of Texas Southwestern Medical School, has described this syndrome as follows:

> Many people in their teens and 20s feel immortal, and sometimes they do foolish things that put their health, or lives, at risk. Although the potential for harm is real, most teens don't really think about the consequences. Still, some consciously take part in hazardous activities on a daily basis.[16]

Sparkman writes that there are those who "live for the chance to indulge in every sort of reckless behavior imaginable," and that such reckless behavior can "lead to other problem behaviors such as drug and alcohol abuse, delinquency, and promiscuity."[17] Sparkman states that some of the problem may be due to a teenager's changes in growth, mood, behavior and self-perception. He believes that while some choose to excel in things such as sports, or their studies, others "desperately seek attention by joining anti-social activities that make them stand out or appear rebellious."[18]

Laura Kann of the U.S. Centers for Disease Control and Prevention agrees. "Too many kids practice behavior that put them at risk of morbidity and mortality—homicide, suicide, motor vehicle crashes, unintended pregnancy, sexually transmitted diseases and, of course, HIV/AIDS," she warns.[19] The article goes on to state that illegal drugs are a significant part of this risky behavior.

A second possible reason why many young people seem impervious to the message that drugs are dangerous is that the debilitation of the mind through drug abuse is a very slow, unnoticeable process. Most drug users, regardless of age, do not notice the effects of their habit until it's too late. Initially, users fail to notice degraded performance in important activities such as schoolwork. Because the average teenager in the United States is dependent on a parent or a guardian, many teenagers do not realize the importance of education. The means by which they will establish a financially stable future for themselves and a family when they become independent adults is still an insignificant problem.

Third and last, many teenagers generally are unconcerned with the opinions, lectures, and statistics of "grown-ups." Many teenagers today perceive their parents' generation, those who were young in the 1960s and 1970s, as the ones who brought the era of drugs and rebellion into the United States. Mental and physical health, education, and a financially secure future are no more important to many of today's youth than they were to the "flower children" of the 1960s.

But there is one crucial aspect of drug use that does not affect one's mental or physical health, or personal future. Nor is it a rebuke from a grown-up. It is the fact that the illegal sale of drugs finances terrorism and insurgencies worldwide. It has turned many of our streets over to powerful gangs, and has already destroyed the lives of hundreds of thousands of innocent men, women and children.

It is safe to assume that most people in the United States were ignorant of narco-terrorism on the world-wide level prior to September 11, 2001. This was first apparent in the irony of the open, almost prideful use of drugs by the flower children and hippies of the 1960s and 1970s. During the Vietnam War—the first time an anti-war sentiment had a major effect on a U.S. military conflict—many young adults burned draft cards and American flags in mass protests, while, ironically, drug demand in the United States greatly increased. "The new industry (drugs) grew out of a social revolution in the 1960s that stripped away the social stigma associated with drug use. Marijuana became fashionable among young North Americans."[20] In this same era (which extended into the 1970s) drugs were encouraged through movies (*Easy Rider, Superfly*), movie stars (Cheech and Chong), pop songs ("Cocaine," amongst many others), and even band names (*The Doobie Brothers*). Many young adult males even used drugs in order to fail the initial Army physical exam.

But all this occurred at the same time that Cuba's Fidel Castro was implementing his drug trafficking strategy as a tool to further spread the communist "revolution" throughout Latin America, and while America's growing use of heroin from the Golden Triangle was fueling the insurgencies in Southeast Asia. At this time hashish and opium were also flowing into the United States at an increasing rate. These drugs, originating in the Middle East (primarily Lebanon), were instrumental tools for financing Middle Eastern violence and warfare, including the notorious terrorist acts of the late 1970s and 1980s against U.S. citizens. Most drug abusers at Woodstock could not have had the slightest hint that, as they protested one war, they financed other wars through the purchase of their drugs.

The public demonstrations of the "flower children" and other protesters of the Vietnam era set a precedent that was further displayed during the Reagan era. Idealistic young adults and others joined the same (now aging) crowd of earlier decades in protesting President Reagan's Central American policies. Who can forget when, in September 1987, protestor Brian Wilson lost his legs as he lay in front of a train departing the Concord Naval Air Station in California?[21] That train carried weapons headed for El Salvador to help fight the communist insurgency already well-rooted in that nation. Anti-war sentiment became so strong that even Congress declared it illegal for the U.S. government to provide any military support to the Nicaraguan Contras, who were trying to win back their country from communist rule.

Yet illegal narcotics trafficking was at this time escalating terrorism in Peru and Colombia, as well as wars in Nicaragua and El Salvador.[22] Many Americans considered Reagan a warmonger. Yet, one could wonder who provided the greater impetus for warfare to continue?

Americans seem to have a benevolent streak that feels for people suffering worldwide. This can be seen not only in various anti-war protests, but also in popular support for humanitarian operations in places like Somalia, Haiti, Bosnia and especially Kosovo, where Americans accepted the killings of civilians by the mass NATO bombing campaign in order to stop the ethnic cleansing of the Kosovo-Albanian population. Yet Americans allow excessive drug use to continue, thereby financing activities that *cause* the suffering. This irony is particularly visible among young American college students. They are at the adolescent age where people tend to become idealistic and eager to make the world a better place, but their "party" life and "innocent" drug use has not yet ended for many of them. It might be quite a shock for them to find out that their drug "hobby" was financing deaths, domestic violence, and wars all over the world.

An exploratory survey conducted by this author at Louisiana State University in 1998 indicated that public awareness of narco-terrorism could lower drug demand (See Appendix 1, "Public Awareness of Narco-Terrorism and Its Influence on Illegal Drug Use").[23] A text about narco-terrorism, with examples of narco-terrorism, was described to 111 students (drug users and non-drug users,) who were then asked to answer various questions both before and after reading the main text. This survey revealed four interesting results.

First, most students clearly did *not* know that drugs financed terrorism. Prior to reading the test on narco-terrorism, about 25% of the students were *highly unaware* of the relationship between illegal drug use and international violence, and another 25% were *somewhat unaware*. After reading the text on narco-terrorism, these numbers rose to 43% and over 20%, respectively. Less than 5% said they were *highly aware* of the relationship between the illegal drug trade and terrorist/insurgent organizations.

Second, education about narco-terrorism could result in decreasing or even eliminating abuse of drugs from foreign sources. Prior to reading the narco-terrorism text, 47% of the *non-drug users* listed the knowledge of international violence as a reason of *high priority* for not using drugs. After reading the text, over 77% stated that this information would keep them from using drugs in the future. If this attitude leads to a change of behavior, this is good news for those in the counterdrug business. Of the *drug users*, there was a division between the women and the men. 43% of the males said knowledge of narco-terrorism would not decrease their future use of illegal drugs, and 25% said it would have only a *slight effect* on decreasing their future drug use. However, the women were quite the opposite. 42% of the women said that knowledge of narco-terrorism would have a *moderate effect* on their future drug use, and 32% said it would affect them to a *great extent*. 64% of the women also stated that being in a room of drug users who also knew about the narco-terrorism relationship would have an impact on their attitudes toward drug use.

The third result also relates to the issue of women being more affected by education about narco-terrorism than men. Believing this might occur, questions were asked about dating drug users both before and after reading the text on narco-terrorism. The attitudes of women about dating men who used drugs (heavily, moderately, and casually) significantly changed for both non-drug using and drug using women after learning about narco-terrorism. In fact, whereas nearly 33% of female drug users were *highly willing* to date a casual male drug user prior to reading the text, only 3.57% were *highly willing* to date a casual user after the reading. (This should be good news for many parents). In fact, among the drug using females, over 70% were *somewhat unwilling* to *highly unwilling* to date a casual drug user after reading the text on narco-terrorism. This was almost double the percentage applied to this same question prior to reading the text. The numbers were significantly higher against dating moderate to heavy drug users, showing that 92% to 100% (respectively) were *somewhat unwilling* to *highly unwilling* to date male drug users after reading the text. Drug use is often a social activity; in fact, through various conversations with males, this author surmises that men in particular offer to share drugs to stimulate women to sexual activity. If females avoid males who use drugs, this purpose for drug use by males is self-defeating.

Finally, the students were asked if narco-terrorism awareness would be an effective tool in stopping illegal drug use in the United States. Approximately 80% of both users and non-users (and even 75% of the male users) answered *yes* and most comments at the end of the survey were very positive. There were, naturally, a few disgruntled survey takers, one of whom stated: "If this narco-terrorism information were true, the government would have told us about it."

However, research scientists are quick to point out studies of the past that show that there is no necessary correlation between attitudes and behaviors. That is, the students may have said one thing, but might act another. Interestingly, a similar study by Dr. Stanton Glantz and Patrick Jamieson on the effects of smoking was conducted with similar results. About the same time that the Canadian government was putting graphic pictures on cigarette packs, a survey of 600 teens was conducted to see if they would quit smoking if convinced it could harm those around them. The results found that when convinced that second-hand smoke could harm others, it more than doubled the chances that young smokers were planning to stop, or had already stopped smoking. The test results concluded:

> . . . the only significant predictor of planning to stop smoking or having actually stopped was believing that second hand smoke harmed nonsmokers, which more than doubles the chances of planning to stop or having stopped smoking.

> . . . concern with second hand smoke is a powerful deterrent against

smoking and a powerful motivator for smoking cessation.[24]

"The kids were more concerned about the harmful effects of second-hand smoke than they were concerned about themselves," Dr. Glantz, a professor of medicine at the University of California, San Francisco, who led the survey.[25]

A historical instance of a significant correlation between attitude and behaviors can be seen in China's success in their drug war during the 1950s. While it is easy to say that Chinese communist draconian measures eliminated drugs in China, this is not entirely the case. Author and professor at the University of Wisconsin, Zhou Yongming, writes that "Nationalism...played an important role in all anti-drug crusades in modern China."[26] After two centuries of exploitation by foreign nations, the Chinese hated all that was foreign. When we consider how foreign nations, from the British to the Japanese, brought drugs into Chinese society, "it is not very difficult to find a nationalistic narrative that blames foreigners for their role in the making of an opium epidemic in modern China,"[27] wrote Yongming. If one were to take such nationalism in context to the September 11 attacks in this country, and the anti-terrorist attitude now prevailing in the United States, it would not be difficult to induce an attitude-behavior correlation against drug use similar to that which developed in China.

My Louisiana State University survey was only an indicator for behavior from one segment of the population—college students—although it is an important social segment, and drug use is common across college campuses. But the point of the message is simple—drug users are not extensively aware of narco-terrorism (even in our highest-level educational institutes), and need to be informed of the harm they are causing to others, particularly if they are unconcerned about the harm they are causing to themselves. Obviously, those already addicted to drugs may not be capable of stopping their drug use simply on account of an education program, as addiction is caused by a change of chemistry in the brain and the addict no longer is able to control his or her activity without serious treatment (although narco-terrorism awareness may give a greater incentive to some addicts to seek treatment). However, the optimum target audience for this education program, teenagers and young adults, are for the most part drug users who are not addicts.

Based on the indicators of the survey above, in concert with the Stanton-Patrick study and China's success via nationalism, narco-terrorism awareness could have a significant impact in reducing drug use. The primary goals of the education process already encompass half of the paradigms prescribed by Manwaring. First, awareness reduces the outside support of the illegal challenger. As drug use diminishes, so do funds supplying both drug traffickers and insurgents. One might ask if halting the flow of drugs would have a sufficient impact on insurgent groups. These groups have other ways of financing their operations—kidnapping, robbing banks, and blackmail, for example. My answer is that the impact would be considerable. These other methods of gathering funds are practical, but the international drug trade provides far greater access to the capital and arms necessary.[28] The Colombian FARC received $1 million a day in 1996 through drug-related activities, according to the Colombian government.[29] Without that money the FARC would find it much more difficult to finance and supply an army. In line with Richelieu ("history knows many more armies ruined by want and disorder than by the efforts of the enemy"),[30] Paul Kennedy wrote in *The Rise and Fall of the Great Powers:* "In protracted. . .war, the country [or entity] with the deepest purse had prevailed in the end."[31] Guerrilla warfare is definitely protracted war, and traditionally solving the issue of providing and maintaining arms and other logistical support is a major concern of every insurgency. A slowdown in drug trafficking could have a greater impact on insurgent/terrorist organizations than a military operation.

Second, education about narco-terrorism urges the international community to recognize the need for consistent "outside support for the targeted government." No longer is narco-terrorism a country-specific problem. Rather, education highlights the transnational dimension of the problem, presenting responsibilities and challenges to a number of nation-states in a number of different ways. The drug war becomes an international effort.

Third, and equally important, awareness and education will not only have an impact on decreasing drug use, but will establish "legitimacy" (Manwaring's #1 factor) to support stronger counter-narcotics programs. Abraham Lincoln stated: "Public opinion is everything. With it nothing can fail. Without it nothing can succeed." No type of force (especially prolonged, guerrilla warfare) is usually considered legitimate if the public does not support it, and in a democratic government legitimacy is vital. In his highly esteemed work *On War*, Carl von Clausewitz placed much emphasis on the importance of legitimacy. He wrote of the importance of what he called the "Trinity of War," or the balance between the people, the government, and the military. He stated that any strategy that ignored any one of these three would have no effect. The Colombia Plan was heavily criticized because there was "no strategy or public relations campaign for winning public support."[32]

Manwaring emphasizes legitimacy, stating: "The concept of legitimacy is based on the empirical understanding that the primary aim of contemporary conflict is to gain control of the population. . . ."[33] He goes on to say that "every effort in the struggle must be directed at that objective (including stages two and three of the unified strategy). Otherwise, the effort is irrelevant."[34] He further wrote:

> Combatants looking abroad for support—or to deny support—to targeted regimes must understand that legitimacy is a double edged moral issue that will either assist or constrain willingness and ability to become effectively involved.[35]

This became clear to Americans during the Vietnam conflict, when the government lost legitimacy to continue the war. This became even clearer to a new generation on 11 September 2001, as the American government gained overwhelming popular support to fight the war on terrorism. To see America's national will to fight terrorism to the very end, an education program could easily create an anti-drug attitude much like the Chinese did in the 1950s. Today, more than ever, the advantages of the national will to fight terrorism should not be underestimated in our effort to stop illegal drug use, as well as take strong, decisive action in stopping narco-terrorism.

Phase 2: Extradition

Our attempt to understand narco-terrorism leads us to a very important legal issue that must be faced if we are to fight this complex problem with any success. If selling and purchasing illegal drugs finances terrorism and insurgent warfare around the world, are not those who sell or purchase the drugs responsible for supporting security threats against other countries, and should not such people be extradited to those countries? After all, hasn't the U.S. demanded extradition of foreign drug traffickers who poison our streets with drugs? Why should American crimes that affect other nations not receive the same treatment? In this section we examine the legal theories of extradition and how they apply to narco-terrorism.

There are five traditional bases of jurisdiction over extra-territorial crimes in international law. In 1935, the Harvard Research Project developed and codified these principles of extradition.[36] The principles are called the territorial theory, the national theory, the protective theory, the universal theory, and the passive personal theory. The passive personal theory applies simply on the basis of the victim's nationality. The Omnibus Diplomatic and Security Act of 1986 relates to this theory. The act supports domestic prosecution of killers of Americans abroad who intended the offense to coerce, intimidate, or retaliate against a government or civilian.[37] However, the United States more often rejects the passive personal theory, and this theory does not warrant discussion within the context of this chapter (as will be seen later).

The territorial theory allows for a state's jurisdiction over a crime, or the effects of a crime, which takes place within the territorial boundaries of that state, even if only "in part" within the territory.[38] Territorial theory is divided into two components: subjective and objective territoriality. Subjective territoriality occurs when an element of the offense occurs within the state.[39] Objective territoriality takes place when the effects of the offense have an impact in a state different from the one where the crime took place. If no harmful effects actually occur in a foreign country, objective territoriality does not apply.[40] A key aspect of this principle is that "subjective territorial jurisdiction is generally secondary to jurisdiction of the state on whose territory the principal impact or result of the conduct occurred—that is, objective territoriality."[41] Therefore, the offender should be extradited and tried in the nation in which the effects of the crime were felt.

The national principle simply states that nationals are obligated to obey the laws of their sovereign state "even though traveling or residing outside [their] territory."[42] This is derived from the notion of Roman Law that a man's own laws travel with him.[43]

The protective principle, as stated by Blakesley, "is applicable whenever the criminal conduct has an impact on *or threatens* [italics added] the asserting state's sovereignty, security, or some important governmental function,"[44] "even if the offense is committed wholly outside the forum state's territory."[45] The primary difference between the protective principle and objective territoriality is that, under the protective theory, the offense is committed entirely outside the country the crime impacts. Moreover, even if the ultimate crime does not actually occur, but shows the *potential* of danger to national security, integrity, sovereignty, or governmental actions, the protective principle applies over the objective territorial theory.[46] However, there must be a mental aspect to this crime, that is, the violence intended must be designed to intimidate, influence, extort, or otherwise threaten the other state or its security. This aspect will be examined more fully later.

Finally, the universal theory allows any state jurisdiction over particularly heinous or universally condemned acts. These offenses include acts that are normally characterized as terrorism, and there is a growing trend to bring trafficking of narcotic drugs under this theory.

One particular work of legalism—the political offense exception—has provided the exception to the rules of extradition. In 1984, a U.S. district court held that the political offense exception applied to government agents suppressing an uprising, as well as to rebels initiating the uprising, or to any offense committed in civil war, insurrection, or political commotion.[47] However, the European Convention on the Suppression of Terrorism, signed in 1977 under the auspices of the Council of Europe, provided that certain acts are not covered by the political offense exception and are punishable in the signatory states. Such acts include intentionally or indiscriminately attacking innocent civilians.[48] Blakesley points out that:

> Killing an enemy combatant during a civil war or insurrection to escape oppression should not be an extraditable offense. On the other hand, killing a child or other noncombatant or its relative peacetime analogue, even if done to promote democracy or self-determination or to escape from oppression, is terroristic murder, and should be punished as such. It should not be exempt from extradition or prosecution to the political offense exception.[49]

Therefore, the terroristic conduct of insurgent groups such as the Shining Path, the FARC, or the Hizballah should not be justifiable under the political offense exception.

Earlier portions of this thesis showed how illegal drugs enter the United States, and how the profits from this trafficking are returned to the traffickers. If no drugs are sold or purchased, no money returns to the traffickers. As a result, the terrorist-insurgent organizations, which make millions of dollars from drug trafficking, lose that significant portion of financial support. The United States is by far the largest consumer of illegal drugs. Because few governments could match the immense funding terrorist-insurgent organizations receive from drug trafficking, it could be asserted that U.S. drug users are some of the largest, if not the largest, financial supporters of terrorism and warfare around the world.

Blakesley writes:

> Our executive and legislative branches have the responsibility to ensure that no policies promoting violence against innocents are adopted or applied. The Justice department must prosecute or extradite anyone who promotes, *aids and abets* (italics added), or participates in terrorism, even when the perpetrator or aider and abettor is a government agent.[50]

Quite simply, the purchasing and selling of illegal drugs does "aid and abet" terrorist and insurgent organizations. Accordingly, these illegal acts should be examined with theories of extraditable offenses. Two are applicable.

First, under the objective territoriality theory, the purchase of illegal drugs in the United States does have a significant impact in states where narco-terrorism is a problem. If there were no illegal drug purchases in the United States, numerous terrorists and insurgent organizations would have significantly less financial support to conduct their operations.

Second, under the protective principle, the purchasing of illegal drugs in the United States does aid and abet both terrorist and insurgent organizations, which are a threat to a nation's sovereignty, security, and integrity. Gerardo Bedoya, former editorial chief of *El Pais*, Cali, Colombia's largest newspaper, stated this problem best when he wrote: "The narcos have corrupted the state [Colombia], government, and society. They have generated violence. . . . They have discredited us before the world."[51]

As to the mental aspect required for the protective principle theory, as mentioned earlier, if the crime is not intended to intimidate, influence, extort, or otherwise threaten the other state or its security, it does not fall under this principle. However, if the people of the United States were informed on narco-terrorism and its effects, as should be the case, then disregard for the impact of purchasing illegal drugs would be a malignant disregard for human life. Such disregard could fall under "depraved-heart murder," which can be defined as:

> Extremely negligent conduct, which creates what a reasonable man would realize to be not only an unjustifiable but also a very high degree of risk of death or serious bodily injury to another or to others—though unaccompanied by any intent to kill or do serious bodily injury—and which actually causes the death of another, may constitute murder.[52]

Once again, education about narco-terrorism must be required because the "realization of the risk" (the support of terrorism) is necessary for "depraved-heart murder" in most cases. In this definition of murder, the requirement of purchasing drugs with the mental intent of supporting terrorism, as the protective principle requires, becomes moot. As long as one understands the potential results of his actions, and still displays negligent conduct, his acts constitute "depraved-heart murder."

The definition of a depraved mind found in Black's Law Dictionary further supports this argument. By Black's definition, a depraved mind is "a mind which may become inflamed by liquor and passion to such a degree that it ceases to care for human life or safety." A drug addict who is aware of narco-terrorism could fall under the category of possessing a depraved mind. So could a person who simply wants to use drugs and does not care about the impact his drug use has on others in a foreign country. Such an irresponsible disregard for human life could be considered "extremely negligent conduct" and, therefore, an act of "depraved-heart murder."

Purchasing and selling illegal drugs does aid and abet particularly heinous and universally condemned acts, that is, the terrorism discussed above. This falls under the universal theory of extradition.

Finally, a U.S. citizen aids and abets terrorism even when purchasing drugs trafficked illegally overseas in states which tolerate drug use. Here, the national theory also applies.

In the case of *U.S. v. Layton*, defendant Larry Layton was found guilty (among other things) of "aiding and abetting" the murder of an internationally protected person (a U.S. congressman).[53] Under this ruling, both the theories of objective territoriality and protective principle applied. If aiding and abetting a murder in this case applies, then what about the millions of drug users in the United States who financially support terrorism and insurgent warfare, thereby impacting a foreign nation's security and sovereignty as well as simply supporting murder? Clearly, these people must be held accountable for their actions.

Some could argue that trying to extradite all the drug offenders in the United States is ludicrous, and perhaps such a discussion is more theoretical than practical. For example, would drug-producing countries such as Colombia even want our common drug offenders? Do these countries have enough prison space for them? Would U.S. offenders have basic human rights that U.S. citizens normally demand? What would it cost financially? Perhaps we should only extradite the "big fish" who traffic drugs, such as those who received presidential pardons in January of 2001.[54]

To answer the first question, countries that suffer from narco-terrorism would need to understand that criminal punishment for the above offenses is not only theoretically applicable, but could be a key strategy in lowering drug use. During the Louisiana State Survey on narco-terrorism awareness, discussed above, the students were asked the following question:

Hypothetically imagine that you, as an illegal drug user in the United States (whether you are or not),[55] now could be prosecuted under international law for financially supporting international terrorism if caught using or purchasing illegal drugs, and could be sent (extradited) to a foreign country to serve time in their prison system, under their rules. To what extent would this prevent you from using illegal drugs in the future?

a. NOT AT ALL____

b. SLIGHTLY____

c. MODERATELY____

d. A GREAT EXTENT____

78% of the students replied "a great extent;" 11% replied "moderately;" 5% replied "slightly;" and 6% replied "not at all." While this was just a theoretical study, the indications for lowering drug demand are clearly present. Even a mid-level member of a well-known gang, and a drug distributor, stated that such a strategy would have a great impact on decreasing her illegal drug activities.[56] Countries that suffer from narco-terrorism need to understand the possible impact that such an extradition strategy could have on lowering drug demand. Affected countries such as Colombia are the ones that should request such extradition. If they would, drug demand could decrease significantly.

The second question considers the potential lack of prison space for these drug offenders. This can be answered in two ways. First of all, if the above strategy lowers demand for drugs (as seems possible), additional prison space would not be required. Second, extradition should be reserved for drug distributors, dealers, or repeat offenders. Some would consider the extradition of a first-time drug user who coincidentally got caught too harsh a penalty. Besides, new domestic laws could apply to first-time offenders. The Antiterrorism and Effective Death Penalty Act of 1996 prohibits funding for terrorism. The act states that:

> Whoever, within the United States or subject to the jurisdiction of the United States, knowingly provides material support or resources to a foreign terrorist organization or attempts or conspires to do so, shall be fined under this title or imprisoned not more than 10 years, or both.[57]

"Knowingly provides materials" is a key to this passage. Education about narco-terrorism is important to make this law work.

The United States may also need to support any country that receives these criminals by helping fund additional prison space. Why the United States? If the United States is responsible for financing so much of the problem, it should probably accept the responsibility for financing some of the solution.

The final question regards human rights guarantees for U.S. citizens in foreign prisons. Although human rights should be observed for every criminal in any prison, the illegal drug criminal needs to understand the consequences of serving a sentence in a foreign country, i.e., that human rights guarantees may be difficult to enforce on a continual basis. However, regardless of the difficult questions which arise in reference to extradition of supporters of terrorism, drug users must still be held accountable for their crimes against foreign peoples.[58]

Prior to implementing an extradition strategy, the U.S. government must provide awareness of narco-terrorism to the public, so the people can understand why such extradition is possible. But the country must also avoid a "McCarthyism" attitude toward this problem. American judges, and the American people, should handle such extradition matters with care and delicacy.

Many may find the idea of extraditing U.S. citizens to a foreign state for any reason as wrongful. But why should U.S. citizens be above international law, while the rest of the world is not? Blakesley writes:

> When we participate in, accept, or acquiesce in the oppression or the slaughter of innocents, no matter how lofty the articulated end, we simply become oppressors or slaughters of innocents....International law condemns it, no matter who is responsible.[59]

The people of the United States have always claimed to abhor needless killing and terrorism, yet America's drug users finance it more than any other people. America's un-persuasive domestic commitment and effort is highly visible and not taken lightly by countries such as Colombia. That country was "de-certified" by the Clinton administration for not putting enough effort into fighting drugs, and therefore lost a significant amount of financial aid. Yet the Colombian people have endured probably the worst horrors that any country has faced in the drug war. Meanwhile, as Colombia suffers hundreds of attacks—creating a killing rate equivalent to an Oklahoma City bombing twice a month—American drug users "happily and freely pumped their dollars to the killers of judges and policemen as well as thousands of innocent civilians."[60]

Annex to U.N. General Assembly, Resolution 2625 (25) stipulates that:

> no State shall organize, assist, foment, finance, incite or tolerate subversive, terrorist or armed activities directed towards the violent overthrow of the regime of another State, or interfere in civil strife of another State.[61]

Yet one can only imagine the repercussions a smaller country would face if its people committed "harmless" crimes which assisted, fomented, or financed terrorism and insurgencies in the United States. If "aiding and abetting" terrorism is an international crime, extraditing U.S. citizens for this crime should not be found unacceptable.

Extradition is certainly a "stick" that could be used during our time of crises with terrorism, but we should have a "carrot" to go with it. Harsh penalties such as extradition probably could cause some, if not many, to turn away from drug trafficking, but for those who do what are the options? It is easy to say they can get a legitimate job just like anyone else. Can they? The mid-level gang member and drug distributor mentioned above was an eighteen-year-old with barely a high school sophomore education. It is easy to blame her for dropping out of school, but consider her past. When she was fifteen years of age, she was doing fairly well in school, and was already being looked at by a university for a full scholarship in cross-country track. Her intent was to get a degree in business. At the same time her home life was a personal hell. Her stepfather beat her regularly, and her mother did nothing to stop it. She went to both the police and her stepfather's employers, but neither gave her much credence, as her mother would deny the outrage. Before her sixteenth birthday she was forced onto the streets, and living under a bridge. Once in the streets, she was forced to join a gang for protection, and once in the gang her job was to distribute foreign-grown marijuana and some cocaine. In the short time I knew this girl, she talked ceaselessly about getting her GED, and going to the university for her business degree. She had been shot and stabbed on several occasions, and she wanted more than anything to live a peaceful life with a legitimate job. Her lack of education would not allow it. One might wonder how many others are in the same predicament.

There are numerous programs that help such "damaged" teens and young adults to get their lives back in order. One such program is the National Guard Camp Challenge program. This program is designed for 16-18 year olds who have the potential to return to school, but whose home environment would not allow them to remain in their current school—much like our young lady friend. The success rate of the Camp Challenge program is tremendous, not only in helping teenagers get GEDs or high school diplomas, but in helping them become positive citizens in society.

The Camp Challenge program is only one of many programs designed for this purpose. If harsh penalties in drug trafficking are applied for aiding and abetting terrorism, such a "carrot" option to the "stick" may be what's needed to get young drug dealers off the streets and back into society in a positive role.

Phase 3: A Specialized Force

Today both domestic and international law enforcement agencies are the primary forces that fight the drug war.[62] Although U.S. military forces provide indirect support to these Law Enforcement Agencies (LEA), and some foreign militaries are getting more involved (but with problematic effects, as we shall see), on a worldwide basis it is usually the LEAs who take direct action and make the arrests. In Colombia it is the Colombian National Police that lead the government's efforts against drug trafficking, while under the Colombia Plan counter-narcotics unit trained by American military is fighting drug production in FARC held territory. Yet world wide drug trafficking and terrorism/insurgencies are being fought as a separate issue, but is this the best method of operation when drug trafficking, terrorism, and insurgencies go hand-in-hand?

This section takes a closer look at the enemy—narco-terrorism, and the type of force required to handle such a problem. It illustrated the necessity of using a military *structured* force to fight the drug war; the legality of using a military force; and which forces should be used to fight drug trafficking, and under what conditions.

In the opinion of this author, the "direct approach" of force should be a last resort. It is expensive, requires great resources, and inevitably causes some public discomfort. (This is why the legitimacy gained from narco-terrorism awareness is so important, as previously discussed.) However, as we learned in the case of Peru's Shining Path, insurgents and terrorists must first be eliminated before we can eradicate the illegal crops. Phase four of this strategy, crop substitution, can hardly occur in an area where the average peasant is forced to grow crops such as coca, poppy, or marijuana, or protected by the controlling guerrillas in doing so.

In order to understand the drawbacks in permitting *only* LEAs to tackle the drug problem throughout much of the world, we need only look at our own premier counterdrug force, the Drug Enforcement Administration (DEA). The DEA is the only U.S. force allowed to overtly *and directly* participate in counterdrug operations overseas with foreign officials. Yet the DEA, though a superb law enforcement agency that is vital for much of the counterdrug effort, is a police force that was neither created nor trained nor equipped to fight an insurgent-operated (military-styled) phenomenon such as narco-terrorism. Meanwhile the military, the force that is designed and trained to handle a problem of this character and strength, sits on the sidelines providing only indirect support. This is partly due to various interpretations of domestic and international law (which will be discussed later), and also in part to each country's attitude toward domestic use of its military. In the United States, some military leaders fear corruption within the ranks from immense bribes;[63] others do not believe a military force can follow the restrictive guidelines of law enforcement to ensure constitutional rights;[64] and there is a fear that using a military in the drug war would negatively affect a military's preparedness for conventional conflict.[65]

Meanwhile, many countries believe that the use of their militaries in the drug war is undesirable due to fears of military totalitarianism and human rights abuses. Such fears are legitimate, as we have learned from the human rights violations by the military in Argentina, Chile, Guatemala, and El Salvador during the Cold War era. Another common fear, especially among Latin Americans, is that of corruption. A former Argentine Foreign Minister advisor summed up these worries in this way: "What people fear is that if the military becomes directly involved in the drug war, not only will civil rights be threatened, but that majors and colonels will be driving brand new Mercedes."[66] Yet Manwaring states in his paradigm that a government must "foster the military-police capability required to achieve the political ends of [a GAP-type] conflict," such as the drug war.[67]

At this stage we should review some realities of the overall problem. First, narco-trafficking provides much of the financing for terrorist and insurgent organizations, whose principal intent is to subvert or overthrow legitimate, established governments. The relationship between narco-traffickers (the drug lords) and insurgent/terrorist organizations is so intertwined that high-ranking Latin American officials have publicly stated they can no longer distinguish between them. Second, narco-traffickers use terrorism to intimidate and neutralize a state so they can continue drug trafficking activities. The December 1994 Summit of the Americas firmly stated that "national and international terrorism constitutes a systematic and deliberate violation of the rights of individuals and an assault on democracy itself."[68] Under such conditions, narco-terrorism has become a serious national and international security threat.

National security is crucial to a country's existence. In *Hiag v. Agee,* the U.S. Supreme Court stated: "It is 'obvious and unarguable' that no government interest is more compelling than the security of the Nation."[69] The reason is clear. Once a state has lost its ability to secure itself, its integrity and sovereignty are easily violated. For example, when describing the violent, corrupt, and intimidated condition of Colombia, Luz E. Nagle asked "Can the [Colombian] Supreme Court possibly make decisions on extradition that are justified by analysis, logic, and conviction? Or will personal fear and political pressure result in the breakdown of law. . .?"[70] With more than 242 Colombian judges assassinated by narco-terrorists since 1981, the answer is obvious.[71] Colombia can no longer completely secure itself; like a country under foreign occupation, it loses its sovereign ability to govern itself.

Under international law as it has developed and applies today, countries often perceive security geographically, and a threat to security is normally assumed to come from another state. In fact, however, a security threat does not necessarily come from beyond one's borders. Security threats can and often do come from non-state actors, under the conditions Manwaring describes as a GAP conflict.

In the early years of the United States, GAP conflicts were commonly referred to as "imperfect wars," or "armed hostilities that did not rise to the level of declared war."[72] Thomas Jefferson used the military in such an imperfect war when he deployed the Navy to defend shipping from the Barbary pirates.[73]

Since Jefferson's time, the U.S. military has fought more than 100 wars undeclared by Congress. This is not the case, however, of the current drug war. Today this country considers drug trafficking activity as only a crime, and U.S. domestic law, in the form of the Posse Comitatus Act,[74] limits military use in enforcing the laws against such crimes. The Posse Comitatus Act states:

> Whoever, except in cases and under circumstances expressly authorized by the Constitution or acts of Congress, willfully uses any part of the Army or the Air Force as a posse comitatus or otherwise to execute the laws shall be fined not more than $10,000 or imprisoned not more than two years, or both.[75]

But, as earlier noted, narco-trafficking has gone far beyond mere criminal activity. Narco-trafficking terrorists intimidate governments by means of armed attacks and acts of aggression. Narco-supported insurgents attempt to subvert governments in similar ways. Narco-terrorists do both.[76] To understand this problem we should heed what former U.S. president James Madison stated in the Federalist Papers, that "the means of security can only be regulated by the means and the danger of the attack."[77] Many fail to understand that counter-narcotics law officials are fighting highly sophisticated and well-equipped terrorist organizations who enjoy paramilitary (insurgent) support which has the power to neutralize a state. In other words, the security measures being taken against perpetrators of the drug war are far below the "means and the danger of the attack."

As we noted earlier, narco-trafficking looks like and acts like insurgent paramilitary action. Fighting such a complex and powerful element solely with law enforcement officials who have not been trained or have the firepower top respond effectively to such paramilitary-styled organizations has not been successful, nor is it likely to be. Narco-supported organizations like the FARC and ELN have even caused a force such as the Colombian military to retreat. The only organization capable of handling such a complex, powerful and aggressive machine as narco-terrorism is a military with advanced intelligence and technological capabilities.

The United Nations' (U.N.) definition of "aggression" presents another problem. The U.N. defines aggression as the use of armed force by *State against State*,[78] Again, the assumption is nations normally perceive the military as a force which fights other states. Such acts of aggression can include state-sponsored insurgencies and terrorism, but no allowance is made for non-state actors who have the ability to affect a nation adversely. This incomplete definition engenders a global problem. For example, the United States Export Administration Act of 1979 states that the Secretary of State shall notify various government representatives prior to licensing exported goods or technology valued at over $1 million to any "*country*" (italics added) which has "repeatedly provided support for acts of international terrorism." It also states that "such exports would make a significant contribution to the military potential of such a country, including its military logistics capabilities, or would enhance the ability of such *country* (italics added) to support acts of international terrorism."[79] Yet, if one considers the non-state actors—U.S. drug users—who export well over $1 million of financial support (for goods or technology) annually to international non-state actors, and replace the word "country" in the above statements with the words "non-state actors," it becomes obvious that *State against State* aggression is only half the problem. The powerful entities affecting world events are no longer states alone, but also non-state actors.

The world needs to better understand and accept the significance of non-state actors as well as the magnitude of power they possess and the damage they can do, and the required force it will take to stop them.[80] Among many examples, a case in point is Thailand, where crop substitution programs failed because a Chinese Irregular Force (CIF) drug trafficking ring seized control of the involved territory. This powerful drug trafficking organization actually had more resources and brute force than the Thai government, and it prevailed.[81] In Peru, the Shining Path sabotaged numerous coca eradication efforts. In Colombia, narco-guerrillas have destroyed entire counter-narcotics bases such as Miraflores. Law enforcement officials, and even weak militaries, simply cannot stop them. Law enforcement members do have moments of victory, but as one DEA spokesman stated: "We win battles while they win the war."[82] These examples in Thailand, Colombia, and Peru demonstrate that narco-terrorists are far beyond the control of law enforcement agencies and weak militaries. Capable military or paramilitary expertise and power are required to stop them.

During the same survey of Louisiana State University students mentioned earlier, this question was posed to students both *before* and *after* reading the text on narco-terrorism:

> Assuming the United States maintains its policy of not legalizing illicit drug use, do you believe[83] the military should be used in combating international drug trafficking if international laws are observed and human rights protected?
> NO____ YES____

To this question, 79% of the students replied "yes" prior to reading the text, and 89% of the students replied "yes" after reading the text.[84] Such a response is only an indicator among one class of citizens that military force is a possible legitimate option in fighting the drug war.

In the context of this book, this question might be posed as follows: "Can military force be legally used to fight narco-terrorism?" The U.N. Charter, Chapter VII, Article 51 asserts that "nothing in the present charter shall impair the inherent right of individual or collective self-defense if an armed attack occurs against a Member of the United Nations. . . ." Significantly, this is one of the few times that the U.N. does not use the term "State" when discussing aggression. With this provision, the international community admits the right to self-defense in an armed attack without specifying who conducted the armed attack—state, insurgent, or terrorist. John Moore, Frederick Tipson, and Robert Turner, authors of *National Security Law*, state that "the right of individual and collective defense embodied in Article 51 of the Charter applies to secret or 'indirect' armed attack as well as to open invasion."[85] Moreover, Article 42 of the U.N. Charter does not specify *State against State* defense either. This article supports the need for state defense by action of "air, sea or land forces as may be necessary to maintain or restore international peace and security."

These provisions of the U.N. Charter seem to support the legal use of military force to fight narco-terrorism. To use the Colombian FARC as an illustration, former Drug Czar Barry McCaffrey pointed out that "criminal trafficking organizations have done serious damage to Colombian national security over the past few years."[86] Former Peruvian President Fujimori, who moved his military to the Peru-Colombian border after FARC's July 1999 offensive, stated that "if all this process of terrorist advances continues, I do not have the slightest doubt" that Colombia "can constitute a threat to the continent."[87] Since narco-terrorism is both a non-state actor and an international threat to peace and security, this article clearly supports the use of force—military or otherwise—as a solution to the problem.

Moore et al. also support the rationale that an armed attack need not be *State against State*. When discussing the Security Council issue of whether an "armed attack" or "armed aggression" involves the use of conventional armies or covert attack and support for an insurgent movement, they state that "most scholars agree that the test of an armed attack is the intensity of the coercion, not the modality of overt versus covert attack."[88]

The U.S. military has been hampered by the Posse Comitatus Act and the Mansfield Agreement in its attempt to execute actions considered law enforcement issues both domestic and foreign.[89] In relation to domestic military action, the drug war is still a social issue (that is, the United States has the majority of illegal drug users) and military action would probably only make this matter worse. However, if a military force is what is required to handle other aspects of the drug war which occur outside U.S. borders, the United States is the most likely candidate for supporting military operations in the drug war. If this is so, then the U.S. military needs legal authority to conduct such operations within the limits of the law, that is, the Posse Comitatus Act and the Mansfield Agreement. Christopher Donesa supports this. He firmly asserts that "at broad levels, the executive branch, and most scholars agree, that the Posse Comitatus does not prohibit extraterritorial arrests by the armed forces," and that the effects of the Posse Comitatus "stop at the border unless explicitly extended by Congress."[90] Other authors concur:

> Debate focused on the opposition to use the military in situations where organized discipline and tactics of a military force were not required, as for example, in the collection of taxes, service of process, supervision of elections, and in response to labor strife when the task was within the existing or potential capability of state forces....With respect to extraterritoriality, Congress, in the debate, did not exhibit concern about the use of troops in terms of the President's war powers or otherwise in furtherance of American foreign policy.[91]

Donesa went on to state that because such military activities would take place outside the norms of conventional law enforcement, the intent of the Posse Comitatus would not be exceeded. More importantly, Congress has even appeared supportive of using the military to be more active in the drug war.[92]

The Panama invasion of 1989 provides what many believe to be an excellent example of military force used in accordance with U.S. domestic law. However, the Panama invasion does have its critics. President George Bush justified the invasion before Congress to protect shipping through the Panama canal; to protect American lives; install the democratically elected government of President Endara; and to capture Manuel Noriega (under indictment in Florida) whose drug-related activities were seen as a national security threat.[93]

These reasons are technically correct. Prior to the invasion, Noriega declared that Panama was in a "state of war" with the United States and had repudiated the right of the United States to protect the Panama Canal—a territory which the United States still legally controlled until 1999. The day after his declaration, Panamanian forces killed a U.S. serviceman, wounded another, and physically abused a service member and his wife. Even prior to these events, this author knows that much more long-standing, serious and unreported violence had been committed against U.S. military personnel and their families. Noriega's regime was still the incumbent government only because he had physically intimidated and coerced the democratically elected government. To clinch the matter, Noriega had been indicted for drug smuggling. Senator Sam Nunn (among others) supported the invasion by stating "...the President of the United States has enormous power...to commit U.S. military forces where he believes it is necessary for the defense of this country or for the protection of our citizens or for the *enforcement of our laws. . .*

(italics added)."[94] However, one critic, Louis Henkin, claimed that the invasion "eviscerate[d] [U.N.] Article 2(4) 'prohibiting the use of force against the territorial independence or political integrity' of another state,"[95] and therefore the invasion was unjust.

But if we should use Henkin's argument to the letter of the Article, then Allies should have stopped at the German border in World War II; the United States never should have occupied Japan; and President Kennedy had no right to prevent Cuba from accepting nuclear missiles during the Cuban Missile Crisis. Other critics state that alternate means could have been used besides military force to solve the problems in Panama, and that the United States stepped beyond the bounds of proportionality by sending far too many troops. However, it is unrealistic to believe that the DEA could have walked into Panama and arrested Noriega under the indictment for drug trafficking and carried him to awaiting U.S. aircraft without serious incident, especially given the hostile attitude of the Panamanian Defense Force towards U.S. citizens. Could U.S. law enforcement officials have done the same when Noriega declared Panama to be in a state of war with the United States, thereby repudiating the Panama Canal Treaty and using violent measures against U.S. service members and their families, or for strong-arming President Endara out of power?[96] Does one think we could have done the same with Hitler once the Allies stopped at the German border? Surely the laws of proportionality do not mean this. And as Judge Hoeveler stated in *U.S. v. Noriega,* the elected government of the Republic of Panama led by President Endara, which would have been the appropriate entity to object to treaty violations (not American critics), did not do so.[97]

The military had a clear role in capturing Noriega—a law enforcement issue which required military force to accomplish—but Panama had also declared a "state of war" with the United States, so it could be argued that the United States was officially at war. But what if the United States is not officially at war with another nation? Can U.S. employees still execute an arrest? The Mansfield Agreement of 1976 seems to indicate they cannot. However, Sandy R. Murphy states that changes in legislation provide that "...United States officers and employees may not directly effect an arrest, search, or seizure in another nation. However, they may be present and may assist while foreign officials make arrests, and can take direct action if it is necessary to their safety."[98] Murphy also asserts that if the Mansfield Agreement is violated a court is not required to divest itself of jurisdiction because Congress provided no remedy under the act. In other words, there is very little to stop a U.S. military presence from fighting in the drug war outside U.S. borders, as long as it is in conjunction with host nation authorities. As a step in this direction, at the 1990 Drug Summit the United States, Peru, Bolivia, and Colombia signed a joint communiqué stating that each country could use its own military within its own territory.[99]

Finally, the U.S. President has enormous power to use military force, and—despite the lack of authority imposed by Posse Comitatus beyond U.S. borders—some commentators even believe the President should deploy troops in the drug war regardless of Congressional opinion. However, this could be an ineffective option, because Congress has extensive control of funding for such projects. Moreover, Congressional approval helps establish legitimacy in the eyes of the American people. The drug war is not a quick invasion like the action seen in Panama; insurgent warfare is normally a long, drawn-out process. Legitimacy is key in fighting such a war, as ongoing, insurgent-type conflicts have not proven to be popular with the American public (for example, Vietnam).

Historical events have shown us that law enforcement does not have the force, equipment, or training to fight the drug war at its present level, and that a capable military is the only force equal to fighting the resources of this non-state actor, narco-terrorism. We have also seen that legal grounds exist for using a military force depending, as always, on the current mood of Congress and its relationship with the sitting President.

What type of military force should fight this war, and how should it be controlled to prevent constitutional violations? United States units such as the 82nd Airborne Division, the 101st Airborne (Air Assault) Division, and the elite Army Rangers have their place when it comes to providing mass destruction on an enemy target, but an insurgent war in a friendly country is too complex for that.

Unfortunately, conventional minds think of these types of conventional military forces when they consider using the military to fight the drug war. This is why numerous senior military leaders fear military use might result in violations of constitutional rights. Hugo Grotius discussed this issue in the seventeenth century when he wrote" "Nevertheless it may happen that those who wish by force to hinder the enforcement of a right may be killed, not intentionally, but accidentally."[100] Protocol I of the Geneva Convention (1949) requires that military forces clearly distinguish between military and civilian targets. The reason is obvious: no one wants a person to be killed for a crime they may not have committed, or which certainly does not warrant death, yet conventional soldiers are basically taught to shoot first and ask questions later. During the 1989 Panama invasion a "large number of Panamanian civilians were killed or are now homeless as a result of the invasion."[101] The Panama invasion did require the use of a large conventional force,[102] but it also displayed the types of results which could incur using conventional forces in an unconventional, GAP-type conflict. The principle of proportionality, which the Pentagon defines as "[prohibiting] military action in which the negative effects clearly outweigh the military gain" is a key factor in maintaining support and legitimacy from the civilian populace."[103] Sending a brigade of the 101st through the Upper Huallaga Valley, as one of its former commanders recommended, would undermine both the political and social objectives of the war, and the coca would just be grown again elsewhere.

Insurgent warfare requires soldiers to be cognizant of target discrimination, and to possess intellectual thinking, maturity, surgical operating skills, cultural awareness, linguistic skills, the ability to work well with foreign militaries—all this along with the military decisiveness and dauntless aggression required of a combat soldier. President Kennedy, a student of military affairs who took an interest in counterinsurgency with the rising conflict in Vietnam, created one such force—the U.S. Army Special Forces—for the very purpose of fighting a GAP-type conflict. The profile of an average Special Forces soldier from an A-team is:[104]

Age	31.4 years
Time in Service	11.4 years
Education	14.6 years
Married	79.7%
Children	2

This profile differs considerably from the average profile of an infantry squad. The average conventional soldier is much younger, has considerably less time in service, less education, and less maturity. For example, an infantry private could be 18 years old, lack a high school diploma, and have only a few months of experience in the army.

In addition to the Army Special Forces, the army has civic action units and other special operations units vital to counterinsurgency warfare. Likewise, the Navy SEALS are developing many of the skills required for such warfare, and Air Force and Army aviators have a package of special operations forces that would also enhance required special operations. Together these forces are referred to as Special Operations Forces (SOF), the unconventional forces of the U.S. military. President George W. Bush's campaign against terrorism shows an exemplary use of SOF, and as we examine them below we can see why he chose this route.

Among the specialties of SOF forces, and in particular the U.S. Army Special Forces, is the ability to work with and train foreign military and paramilitary forces, whether they be the Colombian army, or the Northern Alliance in Afghanistan. SOF forces are oriented via culture and language training towards specific regions of the world, and are deployed to operate with domestic forces in that region. SOF soldiers often find their counterparts ill trained for the operational tasks at hand. SOF may spend 45 to 60 days assisting in training the foreign force, ensuring they have the discipline and capabilities of conducting and continuing required operations even after the SOF forces have left. This type of operation is doctrinally termed a Foreign Internal Defense (FID) operation, if they are working with the incumbent government, or Unconventional Warfare (UW) if they are working with a group intent on overthrowing the ruling power.

Another reason to use SOF is their acknowledged quiet professionalism. Foreign nations do not like the idea of a large, blatant U.S. military presence in their country. First of all, it makes these nations appear as if they cannot handle their problems with their own military. Second, use of the U.S. military in foreign territories is politically risky.[105] The impression of "interventionism" is often foremost in the minds of many in the Western Hemisphere when U.S. troops are deployed to Latin America, and it can be very unpopular. Third, large conventional forces normally are not culturally aware of the nation in which they are operating. This is a very dangerous factor when we consider that many nations believe the United States makes multilateral decisions unilaterally, and that U.S. forces might be used in their territories without their consent, thus undermining their sovereignty.

However, U.S. SOF have been operating all over the world conducting FID missions with foreign militaries for decades without notice. They have always attempted to stay out of the limelight, ensuring that media coverage for sensitive military operations goes to the host nation's forces. Few know of their presence in a foreign state except the local people, but these locals generally accept the culturally aware U.S. soldiers, who commonly conduct civic action projects which support the local population. (U.S. Army Special Forces are often referred to as the "Quiet Professionals.") In addition, senior SOF leaders clearly understand host-nation sovereignty and work well with foreign leaders to ensure that mutual agreements are made on significant decisions. For example, Colombia had requested surveillance and tracking devices, bomb detectors, and other items to support their counter-narcotics effort. Instead, the U.S. sent eight A-37 subsonic jets. It was a nice gesture, but the jets were of little value because there were no airstrips in the drug trafficking areas large enough to accommodate them. Senior SOF leaders ensure such things do not happen.

By using SOF extensively trained in sensitive operations, instead of conventional forces, U.S. senior leaderships fears of constitutional rights and law enforcement violations are significantly lowered. Because SOF operations are sensitive, Department of the Army directives require that Staff Judge Advocates (military lawyers) are consulted throughout all special operational planning to ensure U.S. law, international law, and traditional law of war requirements are met.

SOF soldiers have legal principles with which they must comply. These principles are distilled from the Hague Convention, the Geneva Conventions, the International Declaration of Human Rights, and the customary laws of war. The Staff Judge Advocate must ensure SOF operators know and understand these principles. The average SOF soldier is mature in age and experience and is likely to ensure that legal principles are honored. Each SOF soldier must understand the particular principles that apply when operating alone with a foreign force, independent of extensive higher supervision. Such maturity also limits the potential for corruption within the U.S. force (although the potential for corruption still exists here as it does in any human organization).

Staff Judge Advocates (JAGs) also assist SOF commanders by serving on targeting panels to ensure SOF targets are legitimate, that the proportionality of the methods used against the targets is proper, and that legal implications are considered in issues of collateral damage. Failure to comply with the laws required of SOF soldiers can result in political embarrassment and criminal prosecution of the violators.

Fighting narco-terrorism is clearly a legitimate SOF mission. Working with foreign forces to counter a security threat is one of the prime reasons SOF exist. SOF do not weaken their military skills by conducting such operations; they sharpen their skills on the very types of missions they were created to execute.[106]

Finally, as mentioned before, SOF commonly work hand-in-hand with foreign militaries. This is significant, as the primary force to fight a transnational drug war would need to be a specially trained inter-regional force. Williams and Williams wrote that "any effort that includes a military component might be more effective without the taint of being solely a U.S. venture, but one in which countries of the Western hemisphere have banded together under the auspices of an international organization."[107]

A report written by a group of foreign officers titled *U.S. National Drug Control Strategy: Impact On LATAM*[108] argued that "through broad, cooperative international efforts we can reduce the foreign drug supply,"[109] while motivating other nations to assist the United States in the anti-drug effort. ("International" should be replaced with "inter-regional" for reasons to be explained.) The officers proposal states that the "build up of an international force to deal with the eradication of the poppy and coca fields, and the interdiction of the drug traffic"[110] would not be perceived as "interventionism" by the United States or a threat to the stability of weak democracies. The officers believe an international effort will erase the "Yankee Invasion" stereotype which the drug lords exploit when U.S. forces are committed to Latin America (even if U.S. forces are only building a school in an area ruled by drug kings). In addition, an international force would allow political decisions to be made jointly, rather than unilaterally, a type of arrogance of which the United States is often accused (i.e., under circumstances when *another* country's security is at stake, and not our own—unlike our current War on Terrorism).[111] However, military decisions must still made unilaterally by a single commander, ensuring the military has one, unified goal. This is of key importance. One counter-narcotics operation demonstrated the problems of a disunified command. *Blast Furnace* was a combined, interagency operation conducted in Bolivia in 1986 by Bolivian and U.S. forces. Throughout the campaign it was unclear who was in charge of the operations—the Bolivian President or the U.S. Ambassador. The two countries had different objectives. The United States wanted to disrupt narco-trafficking operations, while Bolivia simply wanted to prevent narco-trafficking generals from staging a coup and taking control of the government for a second time. Bolivia had no desire to upset coca farmers, nor to hurt the cocaine business which had become an economic boost for the country.[112]

Besides a unified command, an effective international force requires highly selected, specially trained soldiers able to handle basic law enforcement matters while also operating as a military force. Ideally, the international force should have law enforcement agents with them during operations to handle the more delicate matters of arrests and any other legal issues which might arise "on the ground." However, all members of the force need a basic understanding of law enforcement to ensure individual rights are maintained when law enforcement officials are not present.

Sovereignty is a key aspect of any international operation. An inter-regional force would be required to follow both international laws and the domestic laws of the States in which it operates to avoid threats to the sovereignty of the States involved.[113] However, this force must have the legal authority and power to enter a nation and remove wanted persons where authorized to do so under a regional arrangement sponsored by, e.g., the OAS or the U.N.[114] Narco-traffickers cross international borders at their convenience and will, often to evade capture by a certain national police force. For example, a Peruvian Air Force aircraft could pursue a drug trafficking aircraft only to have the traffickers fly across the Brazilian border into the Amazon "no-man's-land" and get away. Also, narco-traffickers may stop trafficking through one country if operations become too risky, and begin trafficking through another State. A regional force must be able to freely follow narco-traffickers wherever they may go in order to keep abreast of their operations. The force must be able to react immediately without having to go through a long-drawn-out political process to gain permission to enter another State.

Legally, the concept of a regional force is supported in Latin America by Chapter VI, Article 27 of the Charter of the OAS (assuming, once again, the word "State" can also mean "non-state actor"), which reads:

> Every act of aggression by a State against the territorial integrity or the inviolability of the territory or against the sovereignty or political independence of an American State shall be considered an act of aggression against the other American States.

Chapter II, Article 5(f) flatly reads: "An act of aggression against one State is an act of aggression against all the other American States." Chapter I, Article 4(c) declares that the OAS,

> . . . in order to put into practice the principles on which it is founded and to fulfill regional obligations under the Charter of the United Nations, proclaims the following essential purposes: To provide for common action on the part of those States in the event of aggression.

In addition, Article 8 simply states that "the fundamental rights of States may not be impaired in any manner." Multinational forces have been used in such places as Haiti and the Dominican Republic.

The U.N. Charter also supports regional action in such cases. Chapter

VIII, Article 52 authorizes "regional arrangements or agencies" to deal with "matters relating to the maintenance of international peace and security...." and that these regional arrangements shall "make every effort to achieve settlement of local disputes through such regional arrangements or by such regional agencies *before* referring them to the Security Council."

Moore et al. quote Professor Thomas Franck as saying: "In counteracting an insurgency...the victim state and its allies must respond in a fashion sufficiently effective to deter, yet not exceeding the limits of proportionality."[115] Moore et al. add that:

> Nothing could more quickly doom the [U.N.] Charter to irrelevance than to limit defensive options against serious armed attack solely to those of the least military and political effectiveness. Response solely within the attacked state leaves the military advantage with the attacker."[116]

To leave Colombia to fight the political and military battle of narco-terrorism by itself is leaving the State to die.

Chapter VIII, Article 53 of the U.N. Charter reads: "the Security Council shall, where appropriate, utilize such regional arrangements or agencies for enforcement action under its authority." However, the Article continues: "But no enforcement action shall be taken under regional arrangements or by regional agencies without the authorization of the Security Council...," but there is no clear definition of "enforcement action." Does this mean that a regional organization like the OAS requires U.N. approval before it can go on the offensive against narco-terrorism? Several States of the OAS have raised this issue.

In light of Article 51 of the U.N. Charter, Moore et al. comment that regional action in a response to an armed attack does not require Security Council approval, but that an "enforcement action" does. If we look at incidents of terrorism and insurgent warfare (attacking the counter-narcotics base at Miraflores Colombia; attacking children at hospitals in Peru; etc.), these are armed attacks which require defense. Therefore, a regional organization could conduct offensive operations against narco-terrorists as a requirement of self-defense. The term "enforcement action" would apply to situations such as the recent coup in Haiti. However, regions defending against an attack by a non-state actor must abide by U.N. Charter 54 which reads: "The Security Council shall at times be kept fully informed of activities undertaken or in contemplation under regional arrangements or by regional agencies for the maintenance of international peace and security."

A larger issue which has caused tension between globalism (the U.N.) and regionalism (particularly the OAS) is the question of who has primary jurisdiction over regional security actions,—the U.N. or the regional organization. Some regional organizations, such as the OAS, fear that too much U.N. power provides the "Big Five" (Britain, France, the United States, China, and Russia) too much potential to influence international policy to their advantage.[117]

There are equal claims on both sides as to who should have this jurisdiction, but this topic has been discussed at length by other authors, and these discussions will not be repeated here. However, Moore et al. state that there is "overwhelming support for a Charter interpretation that the United Nations has jurisdiction over all matters affecting international peace and security, and that deference to regional jurisdiction is a matter of pragmatic judgment rather than Charter requirement."[118] This interpretation is sound if one considers that the purpose of the U.N. is to "maintain peace and security." If regional organizations had prior jurisdiction of such matters, the U.N. would be an essentially ineffective organization. In such a circumstance, regional defiance would not violate the U.N. charter if the regional charter had different goals. Regional organizations could even war with other regional organizations just as State with State, and render the Charter of the U.N. a secondary and therefore non-binding document. Also, a number of regional States could then ally against a single regional State (for example, the Muslim States of the Middle East against Israel) and ignore any U.N. denunciation.

For these reasons, it is advisable that the U.N. maintains jurisdiction, while also enforcing the Charter provisions of encouraging the settlement of regional problems by regional arrangements. The U.N. should only interfere if regional organizations do not comply with international law or the U.N. Charter, or if the problem spills over into other regions to the extent that a "higher" authority must control the problem between two or more regions. Meanwhile, regional organizations must ensure they obey international law and abide by the U.N. Charter in their operations (such as keeping the U.N. fully informed of activities pertaining to international peace and security). Regional authorities should also maintain the right to defend themselves in the case of an armed attack (whether from a State or non-state actor), but should apply for U.N. support in prolonged operations, such as the drug war. This will help the region obtain international approval, and therefore legitimacy from world opinion for their efforts.

Finally, one must consider the legal ground on which a paramilitary counter-narcotics force has to operate. In *An Agenda for Peace* (1992), the U.N. Secretary-General defined five types of conflict management mechanisms: preventive diplomacy, peacemaking, peacekeeping, peace enforcement, and peace building. The conflict type which pertains to the drug war is peace enforcement. Walter Sharp further divided peace enforcement into traditional peace enforcement and neo-peace enforcement. Since counter-narcotics soldiers could expect extensive combat in the fight against narco-terrorism, neo-peace-enforcement is the mode under which they should operate.

Neo-peace enforcement authorizes U.N. soldiers to "take military action in response to outright aggression, imminent or actual, on its behalf" as authorized in Articles 39-45 of the U.N. Charter.[119] Two examples of such operations include the Korean War and the Persian Gulf War. Like these two wars, Sharp points out that neo-peace enforcement would permit regional counter-narcotics soldiers to act as a belligerent force. "Under these laws, belligerent soldiers are authorized to use force in self-defense and as required *for the complete or partial submission of the enemy.*"[120]

Sharp also notes that proportionality ("which seeks to establish criteria for limiting use of force") and discrimination ("which governs the selection of methods, weaponry, and targets") should be observed.[121] As discussed before, this is particularly important during insurgent warfare. Christopher Greenwood made note of Sharp's comments. Greenwood asserted that as a belligerent force, the Rules of the Law of Armed Conflict would apply to these regional forces, just as they did during the Gulf and Korean Wars. This gives the forces the right to conduct offensive operations, but also makes them lawful targets to narco-terrorists.[122] Yet, overall this protects the soldier. The narco-terrorists would make targets of the soldiers regardless of the laws, but this arrangement prevents the soldier from being hampered in doing his job, and does not leave him as an open target waiting to get shot before he can defend himself.

A specialized inter-regional force would provide both *political* and *operational* advantages. On the *political* side, a single inter-regional force under the control of a single command, the OAS for example, would provide a single unity of effort, as prescribed by Manwaring. No longer would two countries be implementing different strategies at different times, causing a fragmented effort like Operation Blast Furnace. The OAS could provide the primary objective, with the desired "end state."[123]

Second, an inter-regional effort provides shared regional pride. Every nation and government wants to be recognized on both the domestic and international scene for successful operations. Smaller nations tend to lose credit when conducting operations with more powerful countries, and Latin American nations do not want to look as though they were bullied around by the world's only current super power. Through a multi-lateral effort under an international organization, every State involved can take credit for the political and operational successes.

Finally, a multinational effort prevents an increase in the security dilemma of the Latin American arms race syndrome, which exists between Latin American nations that do not share friendly borders. Many Latin American States do not have the logistics and resources to fight the drug war (or simply will not prioritize their resources to do so). Moreover, a military buildup within a specific narco-fighting State tends to make its unfriendly neighbors nervous, as they fear that these military resources may be used against them later on. These unfriendly borders include Peru and Ecuador, Peru and Chile, and Colombia and Venezuela.

The *operational* advantages of employing an inter-regional force, including U.S. SOF, covers the requirement of Manwaring's prescription for disciplined and capable security forces, and enhances the overall intelligence apparatus. The FID missions described above ensure the entire force is trained and ready to conduct the operations assigned to them. Additionally, a unified command enhances a unit's discipline for military action by preventing confusion of conflicting orders from different commands. Additionally, intelligence is more likely to be shared among a force which is working together for the same goal of providing an effective intelligence apparatus. All too often, different intelligence agencies do not want to share intelligence for reasons of personal gain, while foreign intelligence agencies often will not share intelligence based simply on lack of trust. However, from this author's experience, allied officers working together tend to build trust among one another, and want to succeed together. This also reduces the chance of corruption. Everyone involved is literally under the watchful eye of his/her ally and does not want to make their particular country look bad.

Ideally, an inter-regional force should be allowed to operate within the entire region designated as a "threat" zone, that is, when drug traffickers cross international borders, as they often do, this force would not be required to stop at the border, but could continue the pursuit. This power would severally hamper drug trafficking activities as, as mentioned in an earlier chapter, traffickers often use borders to evade capture by a border-locked government.

Finally, and most importantly, this force will be trained to fight the narco-terrorism conflict. Officers and troops will be specially trained on the complexities of this specific GAP conflict. The legal issues mentioned above will be addressed and resolved. SOF soldiers are most likely to ensure that human rights are taught and enforced. Specific tactics will be applied. No training issue should be omitted.

The strategic purpose of this force is threefold. It would be used to attack, first, the command and control structure of the drug cartels, and, second, the active narco-traffickers. The guerrillas themselves would become a third target only if they chose to get involved, as the purpose of the force would not to be to fight a foreign powers insurgency, but rather to cut off the insurgency's financial support. But in countries such as Colombia, where the both the guerrillas and the right-wing paramilitary are already deeply involved in drug trafficking, fighting with both insurgents and paramilitaries would be inevitable. Additionally, this specialized force would be intended to work *with* national police and military forces, not *in lieu* of them.

These attacks must be so relentless as to keep the enemy on the defensive, crippling drug smuggling operations. They must also take away the very incentive of the narco-traffickers—greed. If a drug trafficker cannot have the time, or the life, to spend his/her income, trafficking drugs is no longer worth the effort. Finally, relentless attacks would keep the drug lords and insurgents at bay while implementation of the fourth stage unfolds—civic action.

Phase 4. Civic Action

Any effective counter-narcotics strategy policy must address the economies of Latin American states, and the poverty that exists in those nations, particularly among the farmers. While crop substitution is the seemingly obvious resolution that some governments see as the answer to meeting farmers' needs—and the current Colombia Plan takes this into consideration—in fact the situation is much deeper than that. This section examines how economics plays into narco-terrorism. It explains the relationship between poverty and drug production, and investigates the economic conditions of drug-producing Latin American nations.

Most people in the counterdrug business already know that if every illegal crop were eliminated, for example through aerial spraying, immense inter-state problems for the drug-producing countries would immediately result. Without some type of viable form of crop substitution, many common peasants would have little recourse other than insurgency or crime.

Even today, in order to keep their coca crops profitable, some peasants are moving deeper into the Amazon in the wake of chemical-spraying eradication methods.[124] The drug lords are following suit and are beginning to use native Amazon people to transport the drugs.[125]

It is important to visualize the life of a rural South American farmer. If traveling through southern Colombia, for example, a traveler would begin to notice small huts at the side of the road, or perhaps up small trails. The huts would most likely belong to a subsistence farmer. Each hut is made of wood or concrete. Possibly it has a hard floor (but probably not), with furniture limited to only what the farmer has made. There might be a few chickens, and maybe a dog. Both the farmer and his wife look years beyond their age due to the hard lives they live. The children are thin, and already losing their teeth due to malnutrition. All of them are illiterate; the nearest school is ten miles away, and there is too much work to be done on the farm for schooling anyway.

But what kind of farming is done here? If the farmer chooses to grow bananas, he must walk to the nearest town to find the seed and somehow manage to pay for it (assuming he was not already working on a farm handed down through the family which already had a crop growing on it). He would begin his backbreaking work growing, cultivating, and harvesting the ripe banana. Once he has a harvested crop, he encounters a major problem. He must find a way to transport his crop. Rarely does the average local peasant have the money to hire a trucker to move his produce, nor does he have a truck of his own. Often the farmer has his children carry the crop to the nearest road and try to sell the crop to those passing by. Or he may try to sell some of his crop to a local storeowner. Either way, he would barely survive financially (if at all). He may or may not succeed in providing even the basic necessities to support his family. If the crop goes bad, he must start all over, with the greatly diminished chance of success that that entails. Such is the usual lot of a rural farmer who refuses grow an illegal crop.

But if the farmer chooses to grow coca,[126] for example, the local drug load transports the seed directly to the farmer's land. He may even provide the farmer with a mule and some "advanced" equipment to help plant the seed. The farmer only needs to grow and cultivate the plant. The drug lord buys and transports the product for more than the farmer would receive for other crops. As a result, the farmer has the money to educate his children and provide food, shelter, medicine and good clothing. A "benevolent" drug lord may also get a community of farmers involved, and provide them a medical clinic (with a doctor), a school (with a teacher), potable water, electricity, road improvements, and much else.

Does the drug lord really have a more genuine concern for the poor local farmer than the government? Probably not. First of all, he is wisely providing the farmer with the tools and equipment he needs to be a productive coca farmer, thereby ensuring a larger crop, and profit. Second, the drug lord is also providing himself a security blanket in the local area, by "winning the hearts and minds" of the local population. He is also ensuring healthy farmers with an improved community in which to operate. This strategy of supporting the farmers and the community is far more effective than force. But should a local farmer not wish to grow the drug lords product, or decide to stop after beginning, he and his family face brutal treatments, including torture and death. This author had a personal acquaintance in Peru who explained such an example to me. This man managed to survive an act of terror in which he watched a drug lord torture and kill his two brothers; wires were wrapped around their necks and the ends twisted tighter and tighter until they were decapitated. Why did this happen? His brothers had sided with President Fujimori's anti-drug program, and would not join the other farmers in growing coca. Unfortunately, force or threat of force seems to be the motivation behind many of the rural farmers rejecting the crop substitution efforts in Colombia.

But many drug-producing farmers choose to grow their plants out of necessity, not out of coercion. Therefore, a Latin American nation undertaking an anti-drug program brings great political and economic risks upon itself, as illicit drug production is often a strong part of its economy. Not do Latin American nations generally have the financial capability to regenerate new crop growth for entire regions. The Colombia Plan has an Alternative Economic Development component, but it may not be enough in the long run.

It is easy to point a finger at the governments of the narco-producing countries, and claim that a more responsible government would provide support to such peasant farmers and win back control of narco—producing areas. But as we have seen, winning back territory held by a powerful insurgency, such as the FARC—which has a deeper pocket than the government itself—is not easy. Moreover, the drug producing Latin American states are not financially capable of providing the support these peasant farmers need to live the same lives the drug lords are giving them, particularly if one considers the current level of poverty in Latin America, as well as the expensive wars that are already bankrupting countries such as Colombia.

Colombia's economic efforts over the past decade have been commendable. The government has initiated good market-oriented policies and minimized reliance on trade taxes. Under the circumstances, Colombia is doing remarkably well as a human development nation. However, Colombia has also had difficulties over the past seven years in areas such as budget discipline, national savings, external debt, and currency stability.[127] But not all of this is Colombia's fault. As stated by economics trade expert Dr. Jeffry Schott: "Colombia's erratic economic performance has taken place against a complicated political backdrop of conflict between the army and guerrilla groups, [and] the threat of US drug policy decertification."[128]

Colombia is also a country with a wide disparity between the "haves" and the "have nots." In Colombia the rich get richer and the poor get poorer.[129] Colombia is not alone is this category. In terms of poverty, the number of Latino people living in neediness increased from 120 million to 160 million over the past fifteen years, an increase of 33%.[130] (Poverty is particularly high among Latin America's indigenous population.[131]) During the same time period, U.S. aid to many Latin America nations decreased. For example, aid to El Salvador has declined to less than $50 million a year, down from over a billion during their civil war, while aid to the Caribbean fell 90%, from $226 million to 26 million, between 1985 and 1995.[132] It is important to remember that Latin America's drug war is not jut in Colombia, but throughout much of the hemisphere, including the Caribbean. And while military force could possibly move coca fields out of their current locations, we have seen all to clearly that the problem merely moves to a new location, which still leaves poverty stricken drug-transit countries vulnerable, as the Colombia Plan (for instance) does not cover alternative economic development in the drug-transit countries. While fundamental aid programs in Latin America appear promising to some, "the poor cannot eat fundamentals"[133]—a truth experienced dramatically by our banana farmer.

In the past, Latin American countries have contemplated various economic strategies. Author Gary Wynia describes three primary types of economic development strategies they have considered: conservative modernization, socialist revolutionary, and progressive modernization.

Conservative modernization pursues rapid industrial growth and increased exports through large, modern farms. It also denies governmental redistribution of property and wealth from the rich to the poor. According to the conservative thinking upon which this development is based, government redistribution to the poor drains the economy of its vital resources, hindering productive investment by the entrepreneurs who know how to successfully handle wealth. Under this theory, once the country begins to grow in wealth (i.e., the corporations grow), the poor will gradually absorb it as they enter the expanding workforce. Foreign investment is welcome as long as it contributes to the growth objectives. This is the strategy similar to what President Reagan effectively applied in the U.S. at the beginning of his administration. Once his strategy began to take effect in the mid 1980s, it provided this country with a strong, growing economy for the next 15 years.

The problem with this strategy is, of course, redistribution of the wealth takes several years (depending on a countries economic status when it began), and governments already stricken with poverty would be required to control or repress the lower class during that time. The United States had the capability to handle a conservative modernization strategy in the 1980s without devastating impacts in the first few years, and—though initially unpopular with some—most would say the benefits it brought the entire country over the next 15 years were worth it. In many Latin American countries, however, the immediate effects of this strategy can leave the poor literally starving, driving many to insurgent warfare, or the lucrative industry of drug production and trafficking to supplement their needs. Additionally, as major corporations grow, and smaller businesses expand in their wake, it takes educated people to fill positions within both circumstances. The United States had the education system for Reagan's strategy to take effect, but many Latin American nations still struggle to provide educational opportunities for all their people. As a result, the poor—who sometimes cannot even get a basic education—do not fit in to the fast-paced life of big business, nor can they create their own small businesses. Thus, the wealth accumulates with those who control the large corporations, and the rich get richer, while the poor get poorer.

Socialist revolutionaries take exactly the opposite view. They are more concerned with the distribution of wealth than with its creation. "Accordingly, all property has to be socialized and all wages equalized, ending class distinction once and for all."[134] Schools and hospitals are provided for those who have been neglected. Eviction of foreign corporations is a must, as is severing trade relations with those who have "exploited" them in the past. The goal is economic autonomy. However, this is easier said than done. Few nations possess all the raw materials and can produce all their own consumer goods to achieve such a goal. Socialism also requires continued repression of the upper and middle classes. In addition, socialism requires a large amount of wealth (which is difficult to achieve, as major corporations are stunted in their growth opportunities) in order to allocate capital gains towards competing government requirements, such as national security and corporate growth, while maintaining the people's welfare. In most cases, as in the former Soviet Union, the people had to wait until substantial economic development had been achieved before their conditions could improve, and this never did occur.

Conservative modernization and social revolution both have one enervating flaw: elimination of an entire class in the economic system (at least during the first years in conservative modernization) a situation which could undoubtedly lead to violence and civil war. Progressive modernization, however, does not eliminate any class. This economic strategy has developed primarily from the economic doctrine of structuralism that emerged in the late 1940s. Structuralists "were concerned with the economic and social structures that impeded a region's development."[135] They believed that low growth rates and foreign vulnerability were due not only to shortage of capital, but also to the maldistribution of property and income, thus leading to inefficient enterprises and insufficient consumption. To resolve this difficulty, the structuralists recommended the provision of economic resources to those who could employ them productively, while the national market was to be expanded to make both rural and urban citizens producers *and* consumers in the modern market. This method is conservative modernization and social revolution combined, without any class elimination. Such a strategy allows the poor coca-growing peasant to stop growing coca for survival, substitute an alternative product for the coca, and enter the country's mainstream market economy.

Historical research by author Paul Kennedy has demonstrated the importance of a well-balanced structuralist-type economy. He found that great powers (or any entity) which could not provide a fair balance between "military security for national interests" (defense), "socioeconomic growth" (consumption), and "sustained growth" (investment), were not likely to maintain their "great power" status for long.[136] Progressive modernists understand this, but also consider the political factor that such a strategy requires support from the upper class to provide assistance in redistribution of the wealth.

But in countries at war, such as Colombia, a structuralist society is hard to build. Insurgencies with a strong base of financial support have the economic advantage. In Colombia, for example, the insurgents' key financial base (from drug trafficking) provides a colossal advantage, because the incumbent government must provide the second and third aspects of Kennedy's balance of the economy—consumption and investment—while the insurgents need not be concerned with these aspects. In fact, it is to the advantage of the insurgent that consumption and investment degenerate, and, accordingly, guerrillas make economic targets a high priority. This is both strategic and ideological. First, hindering economic growth limits the resources the government can use to fight the insurgency. Second, repeated attacks against widely distributed targets force the established military to spread its forces to cover numerous vulnerable targets (such as oil pipelines, an especially vulnerable type of target). Third, by demonstrating the vulnerability of the targets, the guerrillas can extort money for protection from industrialists who want to keep their industries functioning. And fourth, such attacks also show the vulnerability of the government in protecting the people, indicating the "need" for a new government. Keeping the poor in poverty is also to the guerillas' advantage. In Colombia, the ELN in particular has made economic targets a high priority. Targets include oil pipelines, major industrial facilities, ranches, mines, and transportation companies. Colombia's insurgency is estimated to have had an adverse impact of well over $1 billion a year since 1990.

The heavy financial obligations of incumbent governments in time of war often lead to a need for acquiring foreign support. In order to build a progressive modernization society in Colombia, large amounts of foreign financial support are required, and this in turn leads to foreign debt.

To avoid such an unproductive economic cycle, many Latin American states turn to conservative modernization methods. This allows the State's economy to continue functioning. However, it also results in a lack of opportunity for the lower class, which fosters revolutions and insurgencies.

Most Latin American states lack the financial resources to independently execute an economic strategy of progressive modernization, let alone implement efforts of crop substitution for illegal drugs. For them the only solution to a successful progressive modernization strategy would be debt-free foreign aid. I once heard a Congressman from Uruguay ask a high-ranking U.S. government official a single, point-blank question when it came to stopping illegal drugs, he said, "how much are you willing to pay for crop substitution?" His question hinted at an accurate assessment of the cost of crop substitution, but only partially to an assessment of the entire situation. He should have asked: "If the U.S. wants to stop drugs, how much is it willing to pay to revamp poverty-stricken, drug producing societies?" This leads to other questions, such as: Does America want to stop drug use merely from foreign sources in the U.S, and therefore America's financing of terrorism? Or does the U.S. want to stop drug trafficking worldwide, thereby preventing *all* illegal drug activities from financing terrorism? If phases 1 and 2 of this strategy are effective by themselves in stopping or reducing drug use in the U.S., do we really need to go into phases 3 and 4, or can we live with demand in other nations allowing narco-terrorism to continue?

This author does not know the total cost of financing alternative economic development programs for all the poverty-stricken nations in the Western hemisphere. However, if one takes into account the fact that the total cost of the drug problem to U.S. society costs more than $100 billion annually—primarily on the basis of lost productivity, and not taking into account the human costs in "lost lives, educational and job opportunities unmet, families torn apart, health care costs, school dropout rates," and much more—the cost may seem worth it.[137]

But if the intent is to crush narco-terrorism completely, the United States—as the wealthiest nation in the world—will be forced to be the leader in assisting former drug-producing nations to rebuild their economic infrastructures and productive bases, ensuring adequate social services, and restoring their regional economic links.[138] This *does not* mean that the U.S. must become a welfare source for poorer countries; certainly organizations such as the U.N. and the OAS, as well as other economically strong countries, can support the U.S. in this role. However, there are measures the U.S. can take to support the effort. One is to progressively eliminate trade barriers and promote the Free Trade Area of the Americas (FTAA). If this regional economic plan is agreed upon, Schott states: "The leaders of the LAC [Latin American and Caribbean] countries" expect to "spur increased investment in their economies, which they consider 'the main engine for growth in the Hemisphere' (Summit of the Americas, Miami, 1994)."[139]

Schott points out that the FTAA could provide four significant advantages for Latin America. The FTTA would:

> 1) Help promote economic growth by spurring competition in domestic and foreign sources, which would also promote transparency of public policies and contribute to efforts to combat corruption.[140] It would also promote increased trade and investment by eliminating trade barriers and standardizing customs and other national trade practices.
> 2) Provide an "insurance policy" against new protectionism at home and abroad, and also reinforce national economic reforms, making these LAC countries more attractive to foreign investors.
> 3) Make regional infrastructure projects more viable and thus strengthen economic linkages between partner countries.
> 4) Strengthen each LAC country's interest in economic health and political stability.[141]

Obviously, not all countries would enter the FTAA immediately or at the same time, as some countries simply would not provide an advantage to either side if they entered into an FTAA today. "In some cases," Schott notes, "LAC countries will need technical and financial assistance from developed countries to train officials and modernize administrative procedures." But some countries, certainly Colombia if it can end its civil war, could soon be ready.

Many in the United States are already opposed to the FTAA, believing it would hurt U.S. industry. In fact, until only recently the United States maintained some trade barriers with Latin American countries—which these nations saw as contradictory and hypocritical to the counterdrug effort. In August 2001, the United States agreed to renew the Andean Trade Preference Act, but eliminated some earlier trade restrictions in textiles and clothing for drug-producing countries such as Colombia, Peru, Bolivia, and Ecuador. Further elimination of trade restrictions over time, as prescribed by the FTAA, could prove to have long-term advantages, as the "United States benefits when its neighbors prosper and democratic processes take root," and "the FTAA clearly reinforces the economic and political reforms that have already been achieved throughout Latin America."[142] Without such initiatives, economic growth in LAC countries could be stunted, causing even greater unrest within their borders, and possibly enabling insurgent forces to gain a greater foothold in Latin America. And while other opponents might point out what was mentioned in an earlier chapter, that "what NAFTA did for trade it also did for drug trafficking," it should be noted that with phases 1 and 2 of the strategy in effect, drug trafficking from international sources should be much lower.

Three results could be expected from combined crop substitution and economic growth programs. First, providing for the lower class peasants increases the legitimacy of the local and national governments for the poor (and the international community). The peasants will see their governments as not only responding to their needs, but as strong enough to do so. Second, in return, the local population is likely to provide support to the government, and turn against the drug lords and insurgencies (as their alliances are often made out of coercion or necessity). Third, such a dual program reduces the production of illegal drugs, which in turn means less drugs for illegal use.

Crop substitution is an important part of winning the drug war and preventing terrorist organizations from obtaining revenues from the drug trade. However, the situation requires more than just giving a peasant a new crop—it involves entirely new economic opportunities for major drug-producing countries.

Chapter 5

Conclusion

As elaborated in the previous chapter, if the intent of the United States is to defeat narco-terrorism as a whole, than the most important aspect of the *Unified Strategy* is that neither phase of the operation should operate alone. The financing of terrorism via illegal drug revenues must be attacked on all fronts.

Each phase of this concept is intended to complement the others. Educating the United States that drug use finances insurgencies and terrorism is intended to slow the demand for most internationally produced drugs,[1] and justly legitimizes extradition for those who aid and abet terrorism, as well as a specialized inter-regional force to actively fight in this international struggle. This force, in turn, will keep drug traffickers and guerrilla insurgents on the defensive and too busy to concentrate on smuggling operations. At the same time, by keeping both the drug lords and on the defensive and pushing back the insurgents, the incumbent government can regain influence in illegal drug-growing areas, allowing civic action programs to be put into effect. This further curtails illegal drug flow into drug-consuming nations.

In a comparable situation, more than a century ago, it was the very determined General U.S. Grant who, after taking command of the mighty, yet decentralized Union forces, planned an overall strategy in which the different armies would no longer operate "independently and without concert."[2] He used all the Union forces together in one grand strategy to bring down an enemy the North had begun to believe was unbeatable. He sent General Sherman on a destructive march through the South to disrupt Confederate logistic efforts and demoralize the enemy, while General Meade occupied Robert E. Lee's confederate forces. He also furthered Abraham Lincoln's strategy of civic action by immediately rebuilding the South after the war to restore its social and economic structure. Most important, Grant's accomplishments began when the Union was almost ready to declare the war lost.

One must not forget the lessons learned from that strategic thinker, who saved this nation from almost certain division. Like the drug war, many thought Grant's struggle had become "unwinnable," but a well-developed strategy, properly executed by a man who would not quit, made the difference. Today, we also need leaders with Grant-like determination willing to fight this problem with every legal means, but with some out-of-the-box methods. Perhaps the *International Narcotics Control Strategy Report* (1997) stated it best: "The most powerful weapon in fighting the drug trade is an intangible: political will. A first class anti-drug force, equipped with state-of-the-art police and military hardware, cannot succeed without the full commitment of the country's political leadership."[3] Like the Union Armies of the American Civil War, our powerful community, legal, police and military hardware needs leadership to direct it. In light of the current administration's handling of the War on Terror, I dare say that the capable leadership we need to fight narco-terrorism is in place.

Finally, the alliance of the international community is essential for total success. This is, after all, an international problem, and the United States will not find victory in a solitary effort any more than the United States, Britain, Canada or the U.S.S.R could have defeated Nazi Germany without mutual support. Again, our current administration seems very capable of building an international coalition, even in the least likely places.

Our former (pre-September 11, 2001) strategy of fighting this war has not worked. The time for change is now. The Unified Strategy is not the sole solution, and does not mean that currently successful programs should be eliminated. Drug rehabilitation programs on the domestic side, and the Financial Action Task Force on the foreign side,[4] are credible programs which should be continued. However, the Unified Strategy does attack this dual front war of narco-terrorism on both sides. It attacks a powerful enemy with more firepower than health messages directed to seemingly unconcerned youth, or limited law enforcement capabilities. A writer in *Rolling Stone* magazine, when addressing the issue of needing a new strategy to fight the drug war, stated: "If it were possible to police our way out of this crises, we surely would have succeeded by now."[5]

The people in the United States enjoy their democratic freedom, but democracy is a fragile institution. In a democracy "our vulnerability lies...in the strength of our open society and highly sophisticated infrastructure."[6] If we plan to keep a democracy, our vulnerabilities must be protected to the absolute limit of law and order. Admittedly, many might find my recommended measures too extreme, but to quote Hippocrates: "Extreme remedies are very important for extreme diseases."

Appendix

Public Awareness of Narco-Terrorism and Its Influence on Illegal Drug Use

Douglas J. Davids

Louisiana State University

Abstract

The following exploratory survey was conducted in April of 1998 to examine public awareness of the problem of narco-terrorism and the influence an increase in awareness could have on deterring illegal drug use. This survey was conducted in accordance with the Louisiana State University Institutional Review Board. The researcher appreciates the assistance of Louisiana State University (LSU), the LSU Psychology Department, and Heather Honig, a Ph.D. student at LSU who provided survey method advice to the researcher.

Public Awareness of Narco-Terrorism and Its Influence on Illegal Drug Use

The following exploratory survey was conducted to examine public awareness of the problem of narco-terrorism—that is, the financial profiting of terrorist and insurgent organizations from drug trafficking—and the influence an increase in this awareness could have on deterring illegal drug use. The researcher initiated this research due to the lack of concern by many teenagers on the self-health hazards associated with illegal drug use, even though self-awareness drug programs are currently used to prevent drug abuse. This indifferent behavior has been described as the "high-risk behavior syndrome" (Sparkman 1996). Dr. Dennis Sparkman describes this symptom as follows:

> The teenage years are a time for change in growth, mood, behavior and self-perception. Many teens experiment with these as they seek independence and recognition. Some choose to excel in sports, academic studies and community activities. Others may desperately seek attention by joining in antisocial activities *that make them stand out or appear rebellious* (italics added). (1996, p. 126).

For the survey researcher, this high-risk behavior can also be seen to stem from three additional factors. First, physically, a moderately drug-abused teenage body is still more likely to perform better than the average adult body. Teenagers also feel a sense of "invincibility" when it comes to their physical health and well-being. (Perhaps the best-shown example of this "invincibility" is the failed anti-smoking campaigns of the past decade.) Secondly, the debilitation of the mind through drug abuse is a very slow, unnoticeable process. Most drug users, regardless of age, do not notice the effects of their habit. Therefore, degraded performances in important activities such as school work are initially unnoticed by the user. Thirdly, and somewhat related to the second, the average teenager in the United States is dependent on a parent or a guardian. As a result, some teenagers have not yet realized the importance of an education. How such teenagers will ultimately establish a financially stable future for themselves and a family when they become independent adults is still an insignificant problem. Therefore, for these reasons—in the opinion of the researcher—awareness programs on self-health have minimal significant effect on teenagers, either on starting or stopping drug abuse.

As a result of the above, the researcher wanted to test the idea of informing teenagers and young adults, not about how drug abuse affects the abuser, but about the damaging impact their illegal drug use has on other people. During the passage portion of the survey, the participants were informed not only of the narco-terrorism relationship, but were also given descriptions of atrocities conducted by narco-terrorist organizations.

Prior to the study, the researcher believed that females among the target group would be more susceptible to the narco-terrorist information, as females are stereotypically categorized as more sensitive towards others than males.[1] The males, it was believed, would be more callous to the suffering of others, or would simply reject much of the information. As will be seen, in many cases this appears to be true. If this is the case, the peer pressure from narco-terrorism awareness could break down the social acceptance of drugs, and therefore the social sub-culture of drug users. The importance of this issue will be discussed later.

Method of study

Date and participants. The survey was conducted on 8 and 16 April 1998, at Louisiana State University (LSU), Baton Rouge, with adult volunteers. College students were used for the survey because they fit in the target group the researcher believed would be most affected.

Survey description. The survey consisted of first answering questions regarding drug use, the influence of drugs in the participants' personal lives, and their awareness of drug-related violence. The participant then read a 6-page passage about the relationship between narco-traffickers and terrorist and insurgent organizations, and how these latter organizations use drug money to finance their operations. Finally, the participants were asked questions similar to the first set of questions to see how the information on narco-terrorism changed their attitudes towards drug use. The researcher informed the participants that the results of this survey did not affect any grade for the

---

[1] This is not based on any known fact or previous research.

researcher. Participants were asked to simply answer the questions as truthfully as possible.

The following statistics are from the survey. The results will be divided into numbered sections. A written explanation of the researcher's intentions will be provided first, followed by the actual questions on the survey, which will then be followed by statistical data pertaining to the participants. The statistical data will divide both females and males, and drug users and non-users. It will then provide results of users and non-users regardless of sex, and, in some cases, results of the group as a whole. The information is presented in comparative order, rather than the order in which the questions were asked in the survey. When applicable, data from relating questions asked both prior to and after reading the passage are presented to allow the reader to immediately see the change in results. The questions are numbered to assist in the discussion. We will begin with the biographical data.

Biographical data

    a. Total participants: 111 college students
    b. Total male participants: 27.03%
    c. Total female participants: 72.97%
    d. Average age: 20.13 years
    e. Average education level: 14.53 years
    f. Race: Asian 5.41% Black 10.81% Hispanic 3.60%   White 78.39%
       Other 1.80%

PART I

PARTICIPANT RESPONSES PRIOR TO READING PASSAGE

Personal drug use and purchases

Method. The participants were asked if they had used illegal drugs (other than alcohol) in the past two years.

Results. (See Table #1.) Just fewer than 35% of the females admitted to any type of drug use, but slightly over 53% of the males admitted to drug use. Since there were more females taking the survey, just fewer than 40% of the total were admitted drug users.

Discussion. Even though a very small population of the

LSU students were part of the survey, the results of over 50% of the males being admitted drug user is interesting, and may be the subject of a future study. However, for this survey, the results simply provide a wide range of participants for study.

Amount of drug use for admitted users

Method. Those participants who answered "yes" to the above question were asked the frequency of their use.

Results. (See Table #2.) The majority of the total drug users were on the lower end of the spectrum, with approximately 80% of the drug users using drugs once or twice a month or less. Among the males, however, over 30% admitted

Table #1

Question. Have you used illegal drugs within the past two years? (Not including alcohol if under 21).

NO____ YES____

	Females	Males	Total
NO	65.43%	46.67%	60.63%
YES	34.57%	53.33%	39.64%

Table #2

Question. If yes, how often?
a. ALMOST NEVER____
b. LESS THAN MONTHLY____
c. ONCE OR TWICE A MONTH____
d. ONCE OR TWICE A WEEK____
e. ALMOST DAILY____
f. NOT APPLICABLE____

	Female users	Male users	Total
Almost Never	35.71%	25.00%	31.82%
Monthly	28.57%	6.25%	20.45%
1x2 Month	25.00%	37.50%	29.55%
1x2 Week	10.71%	18.75%	13.64%
Almost Daily	0.00%	12.50%	4.55%

drug use once or twice a week to almost daily.

Discussion. Apparently the majority of the drug users in this survey were not hard-core users.

Drug purchasing

Method. The final question was asked to see which sex was most likely to purchase the drugs, and how often.

Results. (See Table #3.) Over 80% of the total drug users "never" or "rarely" purchased drugs. Slightly over 30% of the male users bought drugs "sometimes" to "usually," while less than 11% of the female users bought drugs "sometimes" to "usually."

Discussion. The males were clearly most likely to purchase illegal drugs. However, these numbers do leave open the question as to who is buying the drugs if the majority of these participants are not?

Knowledge of and attitudes towards others' drug use

Method. Three questions were asked to see 1) if the participants knew someone who used drugs, and 2) whether or not they desired that person to stop using drugs. Question 3 asked participants to comment on why they wished that person to stop using if so desired.

Table #3

Question. How often do you pay for illegal drugs? (Please answer even if you answered "no" to question #6.)
a. NEVER____
b. RARELY____
c. SOMETIMES____
d. USUALLY____
e. ALWAYS____

	Female users	Male users	Total
Never	67.86%	37.50%	56.82%
Rarely	21.43%	31.25%	25.00%
Sometimes	7.14%	12.50%	9.09%
Usually	3.57%	18.75%	9.09%
Always	0.00%	0.00%	0.00%

These questions were designed to see what motivating factors were involved in wishing another person would stop using drugs, and to ensure that no participants were aware of or bothered by another's drug use due to the fact that the purchase of drugs financed terrorism and insurgencies.

Results. (See Tables #4 and #5.) Almost all the participants were acquainted with at least one user. Apparently the majority of the participants would like their acquaintances to stop using illegal drugs. However, only 25% of the males responded that they desire for their acquaintance to quit using drugs.

Discussion. This begins to reflect the researcher's prediction that male users have fewer concerns about the effects of drug use. However, as also believed by the researcher that the females (non-users as well as the majority of the users) were concerned about others' drug use. This sensitivity of the females will be further revealed as the survey continues. All those who desired that their acquaintance quit using drugs made reference to health concerns for the user, possible legal trouble for the user, and possible legal trouble for the participant if caught with the user at the time of drug possession.

Table #4

Question. Do you know acquaintances, or have friends or relatives who use illegal drugs?
NO _____ YES_____

Female	Non-users	Users	Total
NO	15.09%	3.57%	11.11%
YES	84.91%	96.43%	88.89%

Male	Non-users	Users	Total
NO	14.29%	6.25%	10.00%
YES	85.71%	93.75%	90.00%

Total	Non-users	Users
NO	14.93%	4.55%
YES	85.07%	95.45%

Table #5

Question. Would you prefer that these persons did not use drugs illegally?
NO_____ YES_____ NOT APPLICABLE_____ **

Female	Non-users	Users	Total
NO	3.77%	35.71%	14.81%
YES	77.38%	60.72%	71.60%
NA	18.87%	3.57%	13.58%

Male	Non-users	Users	Total
NO	7.14%	68.75%	40.00%
YES	71.43%	25.00%	46.66%
NA	21.43	6.25%	13.33%

Total	Non-users	Users
NO	4.48%	47.73%
YES	76.12%	47.73%
NA	19.40%	4.54%

** Two females and one male answered the question in table #4 as "yes," but answered "NA" in the question in Table #5. The intent was for the "no" answers in Table #4 to be able to respond "NA" in the next question. The three "NAs" were still counted as NA.

Knowledge of drugs and violence before reading the passage.

Method. The participants were asked about their knowledge of drug-related violence both domestically and internationally prior to reading the passage. These questions were asked simply to test their knowledge on the relationship of drugs and violence.

Results. (See Tables #6 and #7.) A large percentage was aware of domestic drug violence, well over 80%. However, the numbers of those aware of international violence was smaller. Less than 50% of the drug users were "somewhat aware" to "highly aware," and just over 50% of the non-users were aware in the same categories.

Discussion. The majority seemed to have a vague awareness of some type of drug-related violence, but as we shall see later the narco-terrorist relationship was not well known.

Influence of drug related violence on drug use.

Method. The participants were then asked to see if knowledge of drug-related violence, whether domestic or international, had much impact on the participant's individual choice to use illegal drugs. This was primarily to see if the "big picture" of the soon-to-be-read information on narco-terrorism was to have any greater influence on the participant than what the current knowledge of drug-related violence had on the participants. (This question was poorly worded, as the

Table #6

Question. To what extent are you aware of any relation between illegal drug use and violence (i.e., domestic violence, gang related activities, theft, murder, deaths of police and other justice department officials)?

a. HIGHLY UNAWARE____
b. SOMEWHAT UNAWARE____
c. SOMEWHAT AWARE____
d. HIGHLY AWARE____

Female	Non-users	Users	Total
HU	5.67%	3.57%	4.94%
SU	9.43%	7.14%	8.64%
SA	49.06%	57.14%	51.85%
HA	35.84%	32.14%	34.57%

Male	Non-users	Users	Total
HU	0.00%	6.25%	3.33%
SU	7.14%	18.75%	13.33%
SA	71.43%	62.50%	66.67%
HA	21.43%	12.50%	16.67%

Total	Non-users	Users	
HU	4.48%	4.55%	
SU	8.96	11.36%	
SA	53.73%	59.10%	
HA	32.84%	25.00%	

Table #7

Question. To what extent are you aware of any relationship between illegal drug use and international violence (i.e. terrorism and warfare)?
a. HIGHLY UNAWARE____
b. SOMEWHAT UNAWARE____
c. SOMEWHAT AWARE____
d. HIGHLY AWARE____

Female	Non-users	Users	Total
HU	26.92%	25.00%	26.25%
SU	19.23%	28.57%	22.50%
SA	44.23%	32.14%	40.00%
HA	9.62%	14.29%	11.25%

Male	Non-users	Users	Total
HU	14.29%	31.25%	23.33%
SU	42.86%	25.00%	33.33%
SA	35.71%	37.50%	36.67%
HA	7.14%	6.25%	6.67%

Total	Non-users	Users	
HU	24.24%	27.27%	
SU	24.24%	27.27%	
SA	42.42%	34.10%	
HA	9.10%	11.36%	

above two answers did not request a "yes" or "no" answer. For this reason, the researcher believes, five participants answered "Not applicable" (NA)).

Result. (See Table #8.) Less than 20% of the non-users responded that awareness of drug-related violence had "no influence" on them, while over 40% of the users responded that awareness of drug-related violence had "no influence" on them.

Discussion. The non-users were clearly more influenced by the drug-related violence than the users. The question did not specify whether domestic or international violence had the greatest impact, or whether the concern over violence was for personal safety, or whether consideration for others was involved. However, the researcher believes that most people are not aware of the specifics of domestic or international violence; that is, how the criminals and victims are actually involved.

Table #8

Question. If you answered "YES" to questions 15 or 16 [the above two questions], to what extent does this knowledge of such violence keep you (or would keep you in the future) from using drugs?
a. NO INFLUENCE____
b. MODERATE INFLUENCE____
c. HIGH INFLUENCE____

Female	Non-users	Users	Total
NO	17.31%	39.29%	25.00%
MOD	26.92%	25.00%	26.25%
HIGH	46.15%	35.71%	42.50%
NA	9.62	0.00%	6.25%

Male	Non-users	Users	Total
NO	28.57%	43.75%	36.67%
MOD	21.43%	37.50%	30.00%
HIGH	50.00%	18.75%	33.33%

Total	Non-users	Users
NO	19.70%	40.91%
MOD	25.75%	29.55%
HIGH	46.97%	29.55%
NA	7.58%	0.00%

Narco-terrorism awareness

Method. The next question specifically asked the participants of their awareness that money used to purchase drugs in the United States is being used by terrorist and insurgent organizations to fund their operations.

Result. Approximately 70% of the non-users and 80% of the users were in some way unaware that purchasing drugs supports terrorism and warring factions.

Discussion. The results indicate that the violence people normally associate with illegal drugs is not related to the narco-terrorism passage they were about to read. This provided the researcher with a sound basis to see how narco-terrorism awareness would influence the participants.

Summary of participant responses prior to reading passage

The above questions suggest the following: Drug users obviously have numerous associates who also use drugs, as drug use is often a social activity with its own sub-culture, but even non-users have a large number of associates who use drugs. A large majority of non-users prefer that their drug-using associates would quit using drugs for reason of health and legal trouble for both the user and the survey participant. A little over half of the female users are more concerned with seeing their acquaintances quit using illegal drugs, while the majority of the male users (almost 70%) do not prefer to see their acquaintances quit. The participants are "somewhat aware" to "highly aware" of drugs' association with domestic violence, and "highly unaware" to "somewhat aware" (with a higher percentage "somewhat aware") of drugs' association with international violence. Non-users are "moderately" to "highly influenced" to stop using drugs due to this violence. The female users are fairly evenly distributed between not being influenced, being moderately influenced, or being highly influenced due to the violence, but the males are much less concerned, as anticipated by the researcher. Finally, a large percentage of the participants (over 70%) is "somewhat unaware" to "highly unaware" of drugs' direct financing of terrorist and insurgent warfare.

Table #9

Question. To what extent are you aware that money used to buy illegal drugs in the United States finances international terrorist organizations and other international warring factions?

a. HIGHLY UNAWARE____

b. SOMEWHAT UNAWARE____

c. SOMEWHAT AWARE____

d. HIGHLY AWARE____

Female	Non-users	Users	Total
HU	49.06%	42.86%	46.91%
SU	18.87%	32.14%	23.46%
SA	30.19%	21.43%	27.16%
HA	1.89%	3.57%	2.47%

Male	Non-users	Users	Total
HU	42.86%	43.75%	43.33%
SU	35.71%	37.50%	36.67%
SA	21.42%	12.50%	16.67%
HA	0.00%	6.25%	3.33%

Total	Non-users	Users
HU	47.76%	43.18%
SU	22.39%	34.10%
SA	28.36%	18.18%
HA	1.49%	4.55%

PART II

PARTICIPANT RESPONSES PRIOR TO READING PASSAGE

Knowledge of drugs and violence after reading the passage.

Method. The next questions specifically asked the participants about their awareness of narco-terrorism after reading the passage on narco-terrorism. They were specifically asked if they were aware of the relationship between terrorist/insurgent organizations and illegal drug trafficking, and if they knew that the money from drug consumers is used by terrorist and insurgent groups to conduct their operations?

Results. (See Tables # 10 and #11.) Here there seems to be no significant change from the earlier awareness question (Table #7) about international violence except among the male drug users. In the earlier question less than 40% of the male drug users claimed to be somewhat aware of this relationship, now 50% claim to be aware of it. When asked earlier (Table #9) about illegal drug activity supporting terrorism, only 12½% of male users were somewhat aware of the activity, but after the reading the passage 25% of male users claimed to be aware of it.

Discussion. Possible reasons for the above changes are that the participants did not understand the earlier questions about international violence and narco-terrorism awareness, or perhaps the subject hit a sensitive nerve among the male users. Possibly male "machismo" would not allow some of them to admit that they were unaware that their activity was harming others, and therefore they were doing something "wrong." If this is the case, that would show the researcher's initial postulate was partially wrong, and that males could be affected by the knowledge of the narco-terrorist relationship.

Influence of narco-terrorism awareness on drug users

Method. The drug using participants were next asked what influence knowledge of narco-terrorist activity would have on the participant's future drug use; that is, would it decrease the participants' illegal drug use? If the passage on narco-terrorism had only to have a slight influence or no influence at all, these participants were asked to explain why this was so.

Results. (See Table #12.) Almost 75% of female users claimed they would be influenced "moderately" or to "a great extent" by this awareness, whereas less than 32% of the male users claimed they would be influenced "moderately" or to "a great extent" by the awareness. On the other end of the spectrum, less than 4% of the female users responded that they would be "not at all" influenced by the awareness, but over 43% of the male users claimed they would be "not at all" influenced by the awareness.

Table #10

Question. Were you aware of the relationship between terrorist/insurgent organizations and the illegal drug activity prior to reading this information?			

a. HIGHLY UNAWARE____
b. SOMEWHAT UNAWARE____
c. SOMEWHAT AWARE____
d. HIGHLY AWARE____

Female	Non-users	Users	Total
HU	43.40%	50.00%	45.68%
SU	22.64%	21.43%	22.22%
SA	28.30%	25.00%	27.16%
HA	5.66%	3.57%	4.94%

Male	Non-users	Users	Total
HU	42.86%	31.35%	36.36%
SU	42.86%	18.75%	30.00%
SA	14.28%	50.00%	33.33%
HA	0.00%	0.00%	0.00%

Total	Non-users	Users
HU	43.28%	43.18%
SU	26.87%	20.45%
SA	25.37%	34.09%
HA	4.48%	2.27%

Table #11

Question. Were you aware that the money from drug consumers is used by terrorist and insurgent groups to conduct their operations?
a. HIGHLY UNAWARE____
b. SOMEWHAT UNAWARE____
c. SOMEWHAT AWARE____
d. HIGHLY AWARE____

Female	Non-users	Users	Total
HU	43.40%	50.00%	45.68%
SU	20.75%	28.57%	23.46%
SA	32.08%	14.29%	25.93%
HA	3.77%	7.14%	4.94%

Male	Non-users	Users	Total
HU	42.86%	50.00%	46.67%
SU	21.43%	25.00%	23.33%
SA	35.71%	25.00%	30.00%
HA	0.00%	0.00%	0.00%

Total	Non-users	Users
HU	43.28%	50.00%
SU	20.90%	27.27%
SA	32.84%	18.18%
HA	2.99%	4.55%

Table #12

Question. To what extent will the above information presented above influence your future illegal drug use (that is, decrease your illegal drug use)? [Drug users only.]
a. NOT AT ALL____
b. SLIGHTLY____
c. MODERATELY____
d. A GREAT EXTENT____

Users only	Females	Males	Total
NOT	3.57%	43.75%	18.18%
SLIGHT	21.43%	25.00%	22.72%
MOD	42.86%	12.50%	31.82%
GREAT	32.14%	18.75%	27.27%

Discussion. As predicted by the researcher, female users were much more affected by the awareness of narco-terrorist activity than male users. Of those who responded "not at all" or "slightly" in the above question most of the answers included comments such as: 1) the user only buys marijuana (which means they missed the point that narco-terrorists do make large profits off of marijuana); 2) one person will not make a difference; 3) they do not actually buy the drugs themselves; 4) they do not actually see the problem; 5) the terrorist will use another source; or 6) as one participant stated, she will no longer use drugs after reading this survey.

Peer pressure from social drug use

Method. The drug-using participants were next asked if using drugs in a social setting in which everyone involved was aware of the narco-terrorism problem would make a difference in their use of illegal drugs—that is, would it make them feel uncomfortable about using drugs? This question was asked to see if the social structure or subculture of drug users could be affected by narco-terrorism awareness.

Results. (See Table #13.) The key result here is that almost 65% of female drug users would be uncomfortable about using drugs in a group if narco-terrorism were common knowledge. Just fewer than 38% of male drug users would be affected, and almost 55% of the total drug users would be affected.

Discussion. Again the researcher's predictions were corroborated. Female participants were considerably more affected than the male participants. The researcher anticipates that common knowledge of narco-terrorism could cause many of the users to mutually feel guilt while using drugs, and possibly even bring up discussions of where their drug money is going prior to actual use. Drug use is commonly a social activity (except among addicts), but the indicator here is that common awareness of narco-terrorism, if presented in the proper way, could bring about a break-down in the social subculture of drug users. This, the researcher believes, could be vital in the reduction of drug use. Additionally, even though the males were not as affected by peer pressure as females, they are probably less likely to use drugs if females are not going to use drugs with them, since drug use is often encouraged as a pretext for sexual activity. Mind-altering drugs, like alcohol, are commonly used by males to stimulate a female's sexual behavior. (This probably explains why more males purchase illegal drugs than females.) If many females would avoid males who use drugs, the drug use begins to defeat this purpose of many males.

Table #13

Question. In regards to question #4, would it make a difference if the people using drugs with you were also aware of the information in the text? NO____ YES____

Users only	Females	Males	Total
NO	28.57%	62.50%	40.91%
YES	64.29%	37.50%	54.55%
(MAYBE)	3.57%		2.27%
(Not answered)	3.57%		2.27%

Table #14

Question. If you do not use drugs, to what extent will the information presented encourage you to remain drug-free?
a. NOT AT ALL____
b. SLIGHTLY____
c. MODERATELY____
d. A GREAT EXTENT____

Non-users	Females	Males	Total
NOT	5.66%	14.29%	7.46%
SLIGHT	7.55%	0.00%	5.97%
MOD	9.43%	2.27%	8.96%
GREAT	77.36%	78.57%	77.61%

Influence of narco-terrorism awareness on non-users

Method. Non-drug users were asked to what extent the information on narco-terrorism would encourage them to remain drug-free.

Results. (See Table #14.) Over 77% of the non-using participants responded that the new information on narco-terrorism would influence them to "a great extent" in preventing them from using illegal drugs in the future.

Discussion. The indicator here is that, even though these participants may not use drugs now, the awareness of narco-terrorism will have a great impact on preventing them from abusing illegal drugs in the future. The chances are probably good that these people would not use drugs in their future in any case, but that would not completely eliminate them from considering drug use in the future, particularly with the pressures of adult life as we enter the 21st century.

Participant involvement in narco-terrorism awareness

Method. The participants were asked to what extent they thought they would use the narco-terrorism information to discourage others from using illegal drugs. This question was asked in order to measure what types of peer pressure they would initiate to discourage drug use through narco-terrorism awareness.

Results. (See Table #15.) Approximately 60% of the non-users indicated they would use the information on narco-terrorism "moderately" or to "a great extent." A little over 70% of the users said they would use the information "slightly" to "moderately". However, the most significant number here was that 50% of the female users responded that they would use this information moderately.

Discussion. There seems to be some motive to apply narco-terrorism awareness as a type of peer pressure to stop drugs. There is obviously more likelihood of this among the non-users than the users. However, several of the "not at all" responses from the non-user group expressed in their comments that they believe drug users would not care if illegal drug purchases supported terrorism and warfare, and therefore why try to inform them. However, our earlier results indicated differently. The 50% of the female users who would use this information moderately shows, once again, that the females are more susceptible to the strategy of narco-terrorism awareness, and, once again, more likely to be the ones to break up the drug users' social subculture.

Table #15

Question. To what extent do you think that you will use the information presented to encourage others (i.e. friends, family) to not use drugs?
a. NOT AT ALL____
b. SLIGHTLY____
c. MODERATELY____
d. A GREAT EXTENT____

Female	Non-users	Users	Total
NOT	13.21%	7.14%	11.11%
SLIGHT	24.53%	32.14%	27.16%
MOD	32.08%	50.00%	38.27%
GREAT	30.19%	10.71%	10.71%

Male	Non-users	Users	Total
NOT	7.14%	43.75%	26.27%
SLIGHT	42.86%	37.50%	40.00%
MOD	42.86%	18.75%	30.00%
GREAT	7.14%	0.00%	3.33%

Total	Non-users	Users
NOT	11.94%	20.45%
SLIGHT	28.36%	34.09%
MOD	34.32%	38.64%
GREAT	25.37%	6.82%

Narco-terrorism awareness as an education tool

Method. The participants were finally asked if they believed that narco-terrorism awareness would make an affective awareness tool in stopping drug use in the United States. Those who responded "no" were asked to explain why they felt that way.

Results. (See Table #16.) Over 80% of the total group responded "yes." Even 75% of the male users agreed to this type of program.

Discussion. The portions of participants who believe this would be an affective awareness program to stop drugs are considerably high. The "no" respondents had several reservations. The majority of the "no" participants indicated that they did not believe drug users would really care that their drug purchases harm others. 25% of the male drug users who answered "no" stated either disbelief in the existence of narco-terrorism (one referred to it as "propaganda"), or that they did not care since the problem did not affect them directly. Therefore, there are a number of males who would not be directly affected by a narco-terrorism awareness program, but, to repeat it again, the peer pressures from society, particularly the opposite sex, may drive them to a change.

Table #16

Question. Do you believe the above information would be a good awareness tool to stop illegal drug use in the United States?
NO____ YES____

Female	Non-users	Users	Total
NO	18.87%	17.86%	18.52%
YES	81.13%	82.14%	81.48%

Male	Non-users	Users	Total
NO	14.29	25.00%	20.00%
YES	85.71%	75.00%	80.00%

Total	Non-users	Users
NO	17.91%	20.45%
YES	82.02%	79.55%

Total group	
NO	18.92%
YES	81.08%

PART III.

BEFORE-AND-AFTER COMPARISON OF QUESTIONS REGARDING NARCO-TERRORISM

Social acceptance and dating drug users

Methods. The participants were asked to identify how the participant accepted a potential dating partner's drug behavior. Each was asked to express the extent of which he or she would date a heavy drug user, moderate drug user, and casual drug user. The exact same questions were asked prior to and after reading the narco-terrorism passage. The tables are presented in that order. The participants were also asked to briefly explain why they chose their answers to these questions.

Results. (See Tables #17a and #17b, #18a and #18b, and #19a and #19b.) There is a distinct unwillingness to date a drug-using partner after reading the passage, even among the male users. Prior to the passage, almost 69% of the male users answered "somewhat willing" to "highly willing." After reading the passage less than 44% answered positively to the same responses. Female users went from almost 33% willing to date a casual user, to less than 4% willing to date a casual user. As the tables show, all factors had a moderate to significant drop in acceptance to dating drug users after reading the passage on narco-terrorism.

Discussion. This portion of the survey revealed a significant change after the participants had read the passage on narco-terrorism. The male non-users seemed to hold a high standard against drug-using partners. Even the male user's numbers dropped on willingness to date a drug user (this is particularly notable for moderate drug-using partners).   This, again, may show that awareness of narco-terrorism touches a sensitive nerve among drug using males, and possibly these answers show the affect this awareness subconsciously has on male drug users.

Key to this portion of the survey is the greater unwillingness of females to date a drug user. The change in numbers is significant. The change of 32.14% of drug-using females highly willing to date a casual user to 3.57% is staggering. From these statistics, drug use loses its social popularity among all groups. This, similar to the question in Table #13, shows that a narco-terrorism awareness program could break down the social subculture of drug users.

Table #17a

Question. To what extent would you be willing to date a person who uses illegal drugs heavily? [*Prior to passage.*]
a. HIGHLY UNWILLING____
b. SOMEWHAT UNWILLING____
c. SOMEWHAT WILLING____
d. HIGHLY WILLING___

Females	Non-users	Users	Total
HU	94.34%	57.17%	81.48%
SU	5.66%	32.14%	14.81%
SW	0.00%	10.72%	3.70%
HW	0.00%	0.00%	0.00%

Males	Non-users	Users	Total
HU	92.86%	18.75%	53.33%
SU	7.14%	62.50%	36.67%
SW	0.00%	12.50%	6.67%
HW	0.00%	6.25%	3.33%

Total	Non-users	Users
HU	94.03%	43.18%
SU	5.97%	43.18%
SW	0.00%	11.36%
HW	0.00%	2.27%

Table 17b

Question. To what extent would you be willing to date a person who uses illegal drugs heavily? [*After passage.*]

Females	Non-users	Users	Total
HU	96.23%	82.14%	91.36%
SU	5.66%	17.86%	8.64%
SW	0.00%	0.00%	0.00%
HW	0.00%	0.00%	0.00%

Male	Non-users	Users	Total
HU	100.00%	43.75%	70.00%
SU	0.00%	50.00%	26.67%
SW	0.00%	0.00%	0.00%
HW	0.00%	6.25%	3.33%

Total	Non-users	Users
HU	97.01%	68.18%
SU	2.99%	29.55%
SW	0.00%	0.00%
HW	0.00%	2.27%

Table #18a

Question. To what extent would you be willing to date a person who uses illegal drugs moderately? [*Prior to passage.*]
a. HIGHLY UNWILLING____
b. SOMEWHAT UNWILLING____
c. SOMEWHAT WILLING____
d. HIGHLY WILLING____

Female	Non-users	Users	Total
HU	86.79%	39.29%	70.37%
SU	13.21%	21.43%	16.05%
SW	0.00%	28.57%	9.88%
HW	0.00%	10.71%	3.70%

Male	Non-users	Users	Total
HU	85.71%	18.75%	50.00%
SU	7.14%	12.50%	10.00%
SW	7.14%	62.50%	36.67%
HW	0.00%	6.25%	3.33%

Total	Non-users	Users
HU	86.57%	31.82%
SU	11.94	18.18%
SW	1.49%	40.91%
HW	0.00%	9.10%

Table #18b

Question. To what extent would you be willing to date a person who uses illegal drugs moderately? [*After passage.*]

Female	Non-users	Users	Total
HU	94.34%	50.00%	79.01%
SU	5.66%	42.86%	18.52%
SW	0.00%	7.14%	2.47%
HW	0.00%	0.00%	0.00%

Male	Non-users	Users	Total
HU	92.86%	18.75%	53.33%
SU	7.14%	37.50%	23.33%
SW	0.00%	37.50%	20.00%
HW	0.00%	6.25%	3.33%

Total	Non-users	Users
HU	94.03%	38.64%
SU	5.97%	40.91%
SW	0.00%	18.18%
HW	0.00%	2.27%

Table #19a

Question. To what extent would you be willing to date a person who uses illegal drugs casually? [*Prior to passage.*]
a. HIGHLY UNWILLING____
b. SOMEWHAT UNWILLING____
c. SOMEWHAT WILLING____
d. HIGHLY WILLING____

Female	Non-users	Users	Total
HU	69.81%	3.57%	46.91%
SU	20.75%	32.14%	24.69%
SW	9.43%	32.14%	17.28
HW	0.00%	32.14%	11.11%

Male	Non-users	Users	Total
HU	57.14%	6.25%	30.00%
SU	42.86%	12.50%	26.67%
SW	0.00%	37.50%	20.00%
HW	0.00%	43.57%	23.33%

Total	Non-users	Users
HU	67.16%	4.55%
SU	25.27	25.00%
SW	7.46%	34.10%
HW	0.00%	36.36%

Table #19b

Question. To what extent would you be willing to date a person who uses illegal drugs casually? [*After passage.*]

Female	Non-users	Users	Total
HU	83.02%	17.86%	60.49%
SU	11.32%	53.57%	25.93%
SW	5.66%	25.00%	12.35%
HW	0.00%	3.57%	1.23%

Male	Non-users	Users	Total
HU	78.57%	6.25%	40.00%
SU	14.29%	25.00%	20.00%
SW	7.14%	31.25%	20.00%
HW	0.00%	37.50%	20.00%

Total	Non-users	Users
HU	82.09%	13.63%
SU	11.49	43.18%
SW	5.97%	27.27%
HW	0.00%	15.91%

When asked why they chose their answers to these questions, some of the participants mentioned the narco-terrorism relationship as a deterrent to the dating, but many did not. Perhaps this was also a poorly worded question, as it should have asked if the narco-terrorism had any significance in their change of attitude. However, the change of numbers does indicate that the passage had a significant impact on their attitudes about others drug use.

PART IV.
ATTITUDES TOWARDS ALTERNATIVE OPTIONS

Extradition for supporting international terrorism.

Method. If the awareness of narco-terrorism does not cause a change in the drug user's attitude, the following question has indicated that more could still be done to discourage drug use through narco-terrorism awareness. The participants were asked: If they could be extradited under international law to serve a prison sentence in a foreign country for "aiding and abetting" terrorism, to what extent would this influence the participant from using illegal drugs in the future?

Results. (See Table #20.) Over 80% of the participants responded that such an action would deter their future drug use "a great extent."

Discussion. The numbers to this question are also significant. Male users seem to be less affected by possible extradition, but their numbers are still high. Of the males who stated in the question in Table #16 that narco-terrorism awareness would not be an effective education tool, 50% of them answered "a great extent" to the above question. Of those male users who answered "not at all" or "slightly," they either had no comment, made comments such as calling the survey "propaganda," or expressed some disbelief in the survey.

Table #20

Question. Hypothetically imagine that you, as an illegal drug user in the United States (whether you are or not) could now be prosecuted under international law for financially supporting international terrorism if caught using or purchasing illegal drugs, and could be sent (extradited) to a foreign country to serve time in their prison system under their rules. To what extent would this prevent you from using illegal drugs in the future?
a. NOT AT ALL____
b. SLIGHTLY____
c. MODERATELY____
d. A GREAT EXTENT____

Female	Non-users	Users	Total
NOT	7.55%	0.00%	4.94%
SLIGHT	1.89%	7.14%	3.70%
MOD	9.43%	3.67%	7.41%
GREAT	81.13%	89.29%	83.95%

Male	Non-users	Users	Total	
NOT	0.00%	12.50%	6.67%	
SLIGHT	0.00%	6.25%	3.33%	
MOD	7.14%	25.00%	16.67%	
GREAT	92.86%	56.25%	73.33%	

Total group		
NOT	5.41%	
SLIGHT	3.60%	
MOD	9.91%	
GREAT	81.08%	

However, as seen before, the female users are considerably affected, again influencing the social subculture of drug users.

Military involvement

Method. This last question was presented to see how awareness of narco-terrorism would provide popular support for military actions against drug traffickers. It asked that, if the United States maintains its policy of not legalizing illicit drug use, do participants believe the military should be used in combating international drug trafficking if international laws are observed and human rights protected? Operations Other Than War (OOTW), or Low Intensity Conflicts (LIC) require almost complete public support in a democracy. A good recent example of a LIC which did not have much public support in a democracy was the Vietnam Conflict. The "drug war" is a good example of an OOTW or LIC type of conflict. This question was asked both before and after the survey, with the second question being changed to "do you *now* (italics added) believe the military..." (See Tables #21a and 21b.) The participants were asked to explain their answer if they were against military use in such a case.

Results. (See Tables 21a and 21b.) There was just under 80% total support for military use in the drug war prior to reading the passage, but this increased to just under 90% total approval after reading the passage.

Discussion. There was a large amount of support for military use prior to the passage, but after the passage the support grew by 10% for the total group. However, some participants actually changed their answers from "yes" to "no" after reading the passage. The reasons given for the "no" answers were as follows. One person claimed to have friends in the military, and did not want to see them killed in the "drug war." Another person blamed the problem on the countries where drugs are grown. Two stated a disbelief in defeating the drug lords, while a third was also "skeptical" the military would be successful, and went on to state that the problem lies with the terrorists, and not the drug traffickers.

Table #21a

Question. Assuming the United States maintains its policy of not legalizing illicit drug use, do you believe the military should be used in combating international drug trafficking if international laws are observed and human rights protected? [*Prior to passage*]
NO____ YES____

Female	Non-users	Users	Total
NO	13.46%	32.14%	20.00%
YES	86.54%	67.86%	80.00%

Male	Non-users	Users	Total
NO	0.00%	37.50%	20.00%
YES	100.00%	62.50%	80.00%

Total	Non-users	Users	
NO	10.61%	34.10%	
YES	89.39%	65.90%	

Total group			
NO	19.82%		
YES	79.28%		

Table #21b

Question. Assuming the United States maintains its policy of not legalizing illicit drug use, do you now believe the military should be used in combating international drug trafficking if international laws are observed and human rights protected? [*After passage*]
NO____ YES____

Female	Non-users	Users	Total
NO	5.66%	10.71%	7.41%
YES	92.45%	89.29%	91.35%
(NA)	1.89%		1.23%

Male	Non-users	Users	Total
NO	7.14%	31.25%	20.00%
YES	92.86%	68.75%	80.00%

Total	Non-users	Users
NO	7.46%	18.18%
YES	91.04%	81.82%
NA	1.49%	

Total group	
NO	10.81%
YES	88.28%
NA	0.90%

PART V
CONCLUSION

The final question asked the participants to provide additional comments. In total, 57.27% had no comments, 32.73% had positive comments, 2.72% had negative comments, and 7.27% had neutral comments. Some of the negative comments referred to the information as "propaganda," or stated that if the problem was real the public would know about it by now, or the CIA would have dealt with the problem by now. On the positive side many believed the information should be publicly presented immediately, and wanted to know why it was not public knowledge yet (one even claimed to feel "naive"). Many merely stated shock and general interest. Some participants wanted copies of the survey to show to friends. Another encountered the researcher after the survey, and was quite excited to discuss the issue further. She wanted to quit drugs, but was under pressure from her boyfriend to continue. She had immediately presented him with the information, but he was very skeptical and defensive.

Several commented on an issue which the researcher has always believed would be key to any successful narco-terrorism awareness program—that the information must be presented visually. To throw statistics and numbers of people killed or harmed by narco-terrorism can possibly raise eyebrows, but, as the Vietnam Conflict showed, one photo of a dead individual shown on our living room televisions brings immediate shock and horror. The researcher is quite confident the statistics presented would have been significantly skewed in the direction of degrading further drug abuse if visual images had been used in this survey.

The conclusive results to this survey are that a well-planned awareness program about narco-terrorism could result in a significant decrease of drug abuse in this country.

REFERENCES

American Psychological Association (1995). *Publication Manual of the American Psychological Association* (4th ed.), Washington DC: Author.

Sparkman, D. R. (1996, September). "Risking it all." *Muscle and fitness,* 57, 9, pp. 123-126. Article describing drug abuse among teenage athletes.

Notes

INTRODUCTION

[1] An insurgency according to the definition in *U.S. Army Field Manual 90-8, Counterguerilla Operations*, (August 1986) ". . . implies a situation where a country is threatened by an internal attempt . . . to overthrow the legitimate government," p. 1-1.

[2] Rachel Ehrenfeld, *Narco-terrorism*, p. 24.

[3] James Adams, *The Financing of Terror*, p. 233.

[4] "Colombian Authorities Link Guerrillas to Drug Traffickers," *Special Warfare* (Winter 1997), p. 37.

[5] Merrill Collett, "The Myth of the Narco-Guerrillas," *The Nation* (13 August 1989), p. 30.

[6] James Morrison, "Targeting narco-rebels," *Washington Times* (15 July 1997), p. 12.

[7] H. LaFranchi, "Colombia Calls Its Rebel Armies the 'New Cartels,'" *Christian Science Monitor* (21 October 1996), p. 6.

CHAPTER I

[1] Louis R. Beres, "The Legal Meaning of Terrorism for the Military Commander," *Connecticut Journal of International Law* 11 (May 1995), p. 9.

[2] *U.S. Department of Defense Directive* 0-2000.12-H, Feb. 1993.

[3] Christopher L. Blakesley, *Terrorism, Drugs, International Law, and the Protection of Human Liberty* (1992), p. 35.

[4] Ibid., p. 37.

[5] Ibid., pp. 17, 20.

[6] Walter Laqueur, "Reflections on Terrorism," *Foreign Affairs*, 65, 1986, pp. 86-88; reprinted in C. T. Oliver, E. B. Firmage, C. L. Blakesley, R. F. Scott, and S. A. Williams, eds., *The International Legal System* (1995) p. 178.

[7] Blakesley, Terrorism, p. 40.

[8] Dan C. Meyer, "The Myth of Narcoterrorism in Latin America," *Military Review* (March 1990) pp. 64-65.

[9] August Nunez, "Murderous Drug Cartels Endanger the Continent," *Los Angeles Times* (October 13, 1989) p. B9.

[10] Ibid.

[11] Andrew B. Campbell, "The *Ker-Frisbie* Doctrine: A Jurisdictional Weapon in the War on Drugs," *Vanderbilt Journal of Traditional Law*, Vol. 23 (1990), No. 2, p. 428.

[12] Department of Defense definition of narco-terrorism online, January 12, 1999, www.mil/doctrine jel/doddoct/data/n/04033/htm.

[13] P. Reuter and D. Ronfeldt, "Quest for Integrity: The Mexican-U.S. Drug Issue in the 1980s," *Journal of Inter-American Studies and World Affairs*, Vol. 34, No. 3 (Fall 1992), p. 99.

[14] Ibid., p. 99.

[15] Andres Oppenheimer, *Bordering on Chaos*. New York: Little, Brown and Company (1996), p. 269.

[16] Warren Richey, "Miami Vice II: the Smugglers Return," *Christian Science Monitor* (January 2, 1998), p. 1.

[17] Juanita Darling, "Newest Cocaine Route to States: the Caribbean," *Los Angeles Times* (April 27, 1997), p. A12.

[18] Douglas Farah, "Caribbean Key to U.S. Drug Trade," *Washington Post*, September 23, 1996, p. A1.

[19] Information provided by the U.S. Department of Defense Special Operations and Low Intensity Conflict section, under the Office of the Deputy Assistant Secretary of Defense for Drug Enforcement Policy and Support.

[20] Sun Tzu, "The Art of War," trans. Lionel Giles, in *Roots of Strategy*, ed. T.R Phillips, Harrisburg, PA: Stackpole (1985), p. 35.

[21] "Peru's Drug Successes Erode as Traffickers Adapt," *New York Times Online* August 19, 1999, www.nytimes.com/library/world/americas/081999perudrugs. html.

[22] Larry Rother and Christopher Wren, "U.S. Official Proposes $1 Billion for Colombian Drug War," *New York Times* (July 17, 1999), p. A5.

[23] Douglas Waller, "A Slippery Latin Slope," *Time* (March 6, 2000), p. 54.

[24] Thomas Hargrove, author and former hostage of the FARC, interview by the author, May 22, 1996.

[25] Initially, the FARC took Hargrove because they confused the Spanish acronym of the International Center for Tropical Agriculture (CIAT), as being that of the CIA. Even after they knew Hargrove was not a CIA operative, they continued to hold him for ransom.

[26] Thomas Hargrove, letter to the author, May 28, 1996.

[27] "Peace in Colombia? This year, next year, sometime...," *The Economist* (April 10-16, 1999), p. 31.

[28] Hearing before the Committee on International Relations House of Representatives, One Hundred Fifth Congress, Second Session, 31 March, 1998.

[29] Larry Rother, "Fishing for Ransom, Colombian Cast Net Wide," *New York Times* (June 3, 1999), www.nytimes. com/library/world/americas/060399colombia-kidnapping.html.

[30] Unclassified information provided by the General Command the Military Forces of Colombia to the U.S. Joint Staff in 1998.

CHAPTER 2

[1] Martin Booth, *Opium: A History.* New York: St. Martin's Press (1996), p. 326.

[2] "The Disputatious Diplomacy of Drugs," *The Economist* (September 11-17, 1999), p. 37.

[3] Ibid., p. 37.

[4] Quoted in Ehrenfeld, *Narco-Terrorism*, p. 24. Ehrenfeld credits Captain R. B. Workman (Retired), United States Coast Guard, "International Drug Trafficking: A Threat to National Security" (typescript, 1984). See also, United

States Department of State "Cuban Involvement in Narcotics Trafficking."

[5] Ehrenfeld, *Narco-Terrorism*, p. 20.

[6] Raymond W. Duncan, *The Soviet Union and Cuba: Interests and Influence.* New York: Praeger (1985), pp. 66-70.

[7] Ehrenfeld, *Narco-Terrorism*, p. 25. Ehrenfeld credits DEA, "Involvement in Trafficking by the Government of Cuba," July 1971, declassified March 31, 1982, p.3.

[8] Ehrenfeld, *Narco-Terrorism*, p. 29, and Brian Crozier, "The Castro Connection," *National Review*, Vol. XLII, No. 4 (March 5, 1990), p. 31.

[9] Ehrenfeld, *Narco-Terrorism*, p. 31. Ehrenfeld credits Francis Mullem, Jr. in testimony before the House Committee on Foreign Affairs, Task Force on International Narcotics Control, "Cuban Government Involvement in Drug Trafficking," February 21, 1984, p. 3.

[10] Additional testimony of Guillot-Lara's involvement with Cuba's "drugs for arms" arrangement was provided by Thomas O. Enders, before the Senate Committee on the Judiciary, Subcommittee on Security and Terrorism, "The Role of Cuba in International Terrorism and Subversion," 97th Congress, 2d session, February 26, March 4, 11, 12, 1982, Washington D.C.: Government Printing Office, 23 April 1982, pp. 2-3.

[11] Ehrenfeld, *Narco-Terrorism*, p. 34.

[12] Brian Crozier, "The Castro Connection," *National Review*, Vol. XLII, No. 4 (March 5, 1990), p. 31.

[13] Ehrenfeld, *Narco-Terrorism*, pp. 35-36.

[14] "Narcotics: Terror's Ally," *US News and World Report* (May 4, 1987), pp. 30-37.

[15] Martin Arostegui, "Castro's Scapegoats," *National Review*, Vol. XLIV, No. 25 (November 28, 1992), p. 34.

[16] Ibid., p. 34.

[17] "Exile files drug complaint against Castro," *Miami Herald Online* (January 7, 1999), www.nocastro.com/ voices/exildrug.html).

[18] Martin Arostegui, "Return of the Godfather, Part II," *National Review*, Vol. XLIX, No. 12 (June 30, 1997), p. 26.

[19] Guy Gugliotta and Jeff Leen, *Kings of Cocaine*, New York: Harper Paperbacks (1990), p. 293.

[20] Crozier, "The Castro Connection," p. 31.

[21] Albert R. Coll, "United States Strategic Interests in Latin America: An Assessment," *Journal of Inter-American Studies and World Affairs*, Vol. 39, No. 1 (Spring 1997), p. 47.

[22] Ehrenfeld, *Narco-Terrorism*, p. 34. Ehrenfeld credits testimony in the "Cuban Government Involvement in Drug Trafficking," February 21, 1984, p. 3.

[23] Ehrenfeld, *Narco-Terrorism*, p. 46, and Gugliotta and Leen, *Kings of Cocaine*, p. 269 (also see photographs in center of *Kings of Cocaine*).

[24] Ehrenfeld, *Narco-Terrorism*, p. 47.

[25] Ehrenfeld, *Narco-Terrorism*, p. 48. Ehrenfeld credits Joint hearings before the Senate Committee on the Judiciary, Senate Subcommittee on Security and Terrorism and the Senate Foreign Relations Committee and the Drug Enforcement Caucus, Subcommittee on Western Hemisphere Affairs, "The Cuban Government Involvement in Facilitating International Drug Traffic," 98th Congress, 1st sess., Serial J-98-36, April 30, 1983: pp. 45-46.

[26] Ehrenfeld, *Narco-Terrorism*, p. 49. Ehrenfeld credits Testimony of Alvaro José Baldizon Aviles before the Senate Committee on the Judiciary, Subcommittee on Security and Terrorism (Washington DC: Government Printing Office, March 1998), p. 35.

[27] In 1832 opium had damaged Chinese society so seriously that even the military was incapable of combat. A sound defeat of the Chinese army by Yao rebels was partially attributed to the fact that "many of the troops from the coastal garrisons were opium smokers, and it was difficult to get any vigorous action from them." (From an essay by Jonathan Spence, "Opium Smoking in Ch'ing China," quoting from the biography of Li Hung-pin in "Biographies of the Ch'ing Dynasty," 1962).

[28] The equivalent of 3.488 billion in 2001.

[29] Iris Chang, *The Rape of Nanking*, New York: Basic Books (1997), p. 163.

[30] Booth, *Opium: A History*, p. 345.

[31] Gustovo Gorriti, "Peru's Prophet of Terror," *Reader's Digest* (September 1992), pp. 93-98.

[32] For more information on the Shining Path see Gabriela Tarazona-Sevellano and J. B. Rueter, *Sendoro Luminoso [Shining Path] and the Threat of Narco-terrorism*, New York: Praeger Publishers (1990).

[33] "A Revolution Peru's Rebels Didn't Intend." *New York Times Online* (August 29, 1999), www.nytimes.com/ library/world/americas/082999peru-revolution.html.

[34] "Terrorismo dejó hasta hoy 131,700 niños en orfandad," ("Terrorism Leaves 131,700 Children Orphans to Date") *La Republica* (The Republic) (October 27, 1993), p. 10.

[35] R. Bonner, "A Reporter at Large: Peru's War," *New Yorker* (January 4, 1998), pp. 31-58.

[36] In the 1980s and early 1990s, 60 percent of the world's coca was grown in Peru.

[37] Richard Clutterbuck, *Terrorism and Guerrilla Warfare*, New York: Routledge (1990), p. 115.

[38] G. Tarazona-Sevellano and J. B. Rueter, *Sendero Luminoso and the Threat of Narco-terrorism*, New York: Praeger Publishers, 1990 p. 111.

[39] Ibid., pp. 119-122.

[40] David S. Palmer "Peru, The Drug Business and the Shining Path," *Journal of Inter-American Studies and World Affairs*, Vol. 34, No. 3 (Fall 1992), p. 70.

[41] D. W. Fitz-simons, "Sendero Luminoso: Case Study in Insurgency," *Parameters: United States Army War College Quarterly*, Vol. XXIII, No. 2 (1993), p. 69.

[42] United States Government Accounting Office (US-GAO), "The Drug War: United States Programs in Peru Face Serious Obstacles" (Report to Congressional requesters; GAO/NS/AD 92-36), Washington, D.C., October, 1991, p. 24, cited in Palmer, "Peru, The Drug Business and the Shining Path.

[43] Peruvian military officials, Yurimaguas, Peru, October-December, 1993. (Information received by the author from confidential sources while working for the United States Embassy in Yurimaguas, Peru.)

[44] Ibid.

[45] Tarazona-Sevellano and Rueter, *Sendero Luminoso*, p. 130.

[46] Tarazona-Sevellano and Rueter, *Sendero Luminoso*, pp. 127-131, and Palmer "Peru, The Drug Business and the Shining Path," pp. 70-71.

[47] Palmer, "Peru, The Drug Business and the Shining Path," p. 71.

[48] Ibid. Palmer credits US-DS, Office of Andean Affairs (1991), 7-section, p. 25a.

[49] "Peru's Drug Successes Erode as Traffickers Adapt," *New York Times Online* (August 19, 1999(, www.nytimes.com/library/world/americas/081999peru-drugs.htm.

[50] Ibid.

[51] Ehrenfeld, *Narco-Terrorism*, p. 87, and Gugliotta and Leen, *Kings of Cocaine*, pp. 411-417.

[52] Randy J. Kolton, Major, "Combating the Colombian Drug Cartels," *Military Review* (March, 1990), p. 53.

[53] Ehrenfeld, *Narco-Terrorism*, p. 74.

[54] Recently the M-19 has stopped operating as an insurgent group and has been advancing its goals through political means as a legal party in Colombia.

[55] Adams, *The Financing of Terror*, p. 217.

[56] Ibid., p. 219.

[57] Merrill Collett, *The Cocaine Connection*, p. 8. (By the end of the 1970s, Colombia was producing 75 percent of the marijuana distributed in the United States. Today it is believed to be much less.)

[58] Barbara Crossette, "War on Drugs Urged at U.N. By Colombia," *New York Times* (September 24, 1996), p. A8.

[59] Douglas Farah, "New Threat From Colombia: Heroin," *Washington Post*, March 27, 1997, p. A1.

[60] Data provided by the General Command, Military Forces of Colombia, to the United States Joint Staff, Pentagon, during counter-narcotics briefing in 1998.

[61] Unclassified information sources from a classified United States Government document.

[62] Michael Shifter, "Colombia on the Brink," *Foreign Affairs* (July/August, 1999), p. 15.

[63] "Warpaths," *The Economist*, (July 24-30, 1999), p. 34.

[64] Lally Weymouth, "Battling 'the Bad Guys,'" *Newsweek* (14 February, 2000), p. 50.

[65] "Latin American Overview," U.S State Department, 27 Feb, 1999, www.state.gov/www/global/terrorism/ 1997Report/latin.html.

[66] Shifter, "Colombia on the Brink," p. 17.

[67] Max Manwaring, "U.S. Security Policy in the Western Hemisphere," *Implementing Plan Colombia* (Special Series), Strategic Studies Institute, U.S. Army War College (June 2001), p. 11.

[68] "Colombian Rebels Kill 24," *Fayetteville Observer Times* (September 21, 1995), p. 16A.

[69] "Rampage By Colombian Rebels Marks New Level of Brutality," *Washington Post* (June 3, 2000), p. 14.

[70] Laura Brooks, "Colombian Insurgents Threaten Elections," *Washington Post* (October 14, 1997), p. A13.

[71] The FARC boasts about 17,000 fighters, while the ELN is estimated to have 3,000 to 5,000 fighters.

[72] T. Johnson, "Rebels Wipe Out Anti-narcotics Base," *Miami Herald* (August 6, 1998), pp. A1, 16A.

[73] Rother, Wren, "United States Official Proposes $1 Billion for Colombian Drug War," p. A5.

[74] "Colombia in the Long Shadow of War," *The Economist* (July 17-23, 1999), p. 31.

[75] Ibid., p. 32.

[76] "Colombian Rebels Kidnap 100 at Mass but Later Let Most Go," *New York Times Online* (May 31, 1999), www.nytimes.com/yr/mo/day/news/world/ colombia-kidnapping. html).

[77] "Messages of War," *The Economist* (May 29–June 4, 1999), p. 37.

[78] "Country Reports: Colombia," *Worldwide Refugee Information* (Decem-

ber 20, 1999), http://refugees.org/ world/countryrpt/amer_carib/ colombia.htm.

[79] "Messages of War," *The Economist*, p. 37.

[80] Anne Proenza, "Le Monde", Paris (January 5-6, 1997), in "Mother of Courage," *World Press Review* (March, 1997) p. 9.

[81] "Country Reports: Colombia," *Worldwide Refugee Information.*

[82] Sibylla Brodzinsky, "Guerrillas Threaten Colombia's Peace Effort," *USA Today* (December 8, 1999), p. 24A.

[83] "Report: Arms Dealers Feeding Burundi War," *USA Today* (August 10, 1995), p. 8A.

[84] "Colombians Dream of Peace," *The Economist* (May 15-21), 1999, p. 37.

[85] Instability in drug-affected nations is normally good for business in the illegal drug trade. During China's Warlord Period starting in 1916, the destabilization in the land gave a major boost to the opium trade, which financed the Warlords domains. The Triads (the criminal organizations that dominated much of the opium trade) flourished during this time of unrest.

[86] "Columbia—Advance of the Russian Mafia," (excerpts by Alirio Fernando Bustos, *El Tiempo) Reserve Officer Association National Security Report* (July 1999), p. 38.

[87] Douglas Farah, "Russian Mob, Drug Cartels Joining Forces," *Washington Post Online* (September 29, 1997), p. A1.

[88] Mireya Navarro, "Russian Submarine Drifts Into Center of a Brazen Drug Plot," *New York Times* (March 7, 1997), p. A22.

[89] "Colombian Police Find Drug Sub," *Join Together* Online (September 18, 2000), www.jointogther.org/sa/wire/ news/reader.jtml?Object_ID=264452.

[90] "Meet the Terrorist International," Wall Street Journal Europe (August 29, 2001,) http://ebird.dtic.mil /Aug2001/e20010829.htm.

[91] "Iranian Investment in Colombia Raises Suspicion," *Stratfor.com, Global Intelligence Updates: Colombia* (December 2, 1999).

[92] Robert Windrem, "U.S. to Sanction Chinese Company," MSNBC Online (June 27, 2001), www.msnbc.com/ news/59039.asp?One=21021110G.

[93] "Pakistan Sponsored Narco-terrorism in India," Papers from the *Indian Defense Review* (12 January 1999), (http://www.geocities.com/The Tropics/3328/idr00007/htm).

[94] "Indian Security Challenged by Narcoterrorists," *Special Warfare* (October 1994), p. 52.

[95] Jerry Seper, "Taliban Threatens to Add Opium to Arsenal," *Washington Times* (September 27, 2001), p. 14.

[96] Jamie McIntyre, "U.S. Considering Targeting Taliban Drug Trade," *CNN.com*, (September 24, 2001), www.cnn.com/2001/US/09/24/ret.taliban.drugs/.

[97] Paul Gahlinger. Interview. "Could the war on terror help reduce the world's supply of illegal narcotics?" *Fox and Friends*, FoxNews (November, 19 2001).

[98] Colin Barraclough, "Iran Confronts a Long-Hidden Problem: Drugs," *New York Times Online* (August 29, 1999), www.nytimes.com/library/world/mideast/082999iran-drugs.html.

[99] Rowan Scarborough, "Global Command Considered," *Washington Times Online* (October 23, 2001).

[100] International Narctoics Control Strategy Report, 1999. Released by the Bureau for International Narcotics and Law Enforcement Affairs, U.S. Department of State, Washington, DC, March 2000.

[101] U.S. Senate, Republican Policy Committee, The Kosovo Liberation Army: Does the Clinton Policy Support Group with Terror, Drug Ties?" March 31, 1999.

[102] "The Ferghana Valley," *Jane's for Intelink* (1 September, 2001), janes.ic.gov/cgi-bin/texis/bin/se ...x_eUqO-?this_edition+jir2001&itemnum=30.

[103] Bill Gertz, "Bin Laden Terror Group Tries to Acquire Chemical Arms," *Washington Times* (September 26, 2001), p. A3.

[104] "Transnational Crime and Terrorism," *Jane's for Intelink* (August 1, 2001), janes.ic.gov/cgi-bin/texis/ bin/se...x_eUqO-?this_edition+jir2001&itemnum=24.

[105] Steve Mufson, "Updated List designates 28 Groups as Terrorist," *Washington Post* (October 6, 2001), p. A20.

[106] Adams, *The Financing of Terror*, pp. 229-233.

[107] Booth, *Opium: A History*, p. 103.

[108] From 1729 to 1767 opium importation increased five-fold. And from 1767 to 1798, it nearly doubled. Zhou Yongming, *Anti-Drug Crusades in Twentieth-Century China*, New York: Rowman & Littlefield Publishers, Inc., p. 13.

[109] An essay by Jonathan Spence, "Opium Smoking in Ch'ing China," quoting from the biography of Li Hung-pin in "Biographies of the Ch'ing Dynasty" (1962).

[110] Yongming, *Anti-Drug Crusades*, p. 15.

[111] Martin Booth, *Opium: A History*, p. 128.

[112] Yongming, *Anti-drug Crusades*, pp. 16-17. Yongming credits Kathleen Lodwick, *Crusaders Against Opium: Protestant Missionaries in China, 1874-1917*, Lexington: University of Kentucky Press (1996). p. 27.

[113] The second Opium War for China was against a Western alliance, which involved British, French, and even some American forces.

[114] Drug Enforcement Administration, "Drug Legalization: Myths and Misconceptions," U.S. Department of Justice (1994), p. 23. The Drug Enforcement Administration credits Gabriel G. Nahas, "The Decline of Drugged Nations," *Wall Street Journal* (July 11, 1988).

[115] Alfred W. McCoy, *The Politics of Heroin*, Brooklyn, New York: Lawrence Hill Books (1991), p. 129.

[116] Ibid., p. 129.

[117] Booth, *Opium: A History*, p. 257.

[118] Ibid., p. 129.

[119] Ibid., p. 277.

[120] Martin Booth, *The Dragon Syndicates.* New York: Carroll & Graf Publishers (1999), p. 168.

[121] "Rancher Tells of Drug Gangs' Intimidation," *Fayetteville Observer-Times* (August 1, 1996), p. 3A.

[122] Carl S. Taylor, "Gang Imperialism," *Gangs in America*, ed. C. Ronald Huff, Newbury Park, CA: Sage Publications, Inc. (1990), p. 103.

[123] [Identity withheld], Baton Rouge, Louisiana, interview by the author, April 16, 1998.

[124] Taylor, "Gang Imperialism," p. 107.

[125] "Tot slain in wrong turn onto 'Avenue of Killers,'" *USA Today* (September 19, 1995), p. 3A.

[126] The Kentucky National Guard FY 2001 Counterdrug Support Plan, Kentucky National Guard Counterdrug program.

[127] "Puerto Rico A Favorite Of Cartels," *Washington Post* (February 16, 1998), p. A22.

[128] Ibid., p. A22.

[129] Martin Van Creveld, *Supplying War*, p. 17.

CHAPTER 3

[1] M. J. Dziedzic, "The Organization of American States and Drug Control," in S. B. MacDonald and B. Zagaris, eds., *International Handbook on Drug Control*, Westport, CT: Greenwood Press (1992), p. 399.

[2] Ibid., p. 397.

[3] Ibid., p. 400.

[4] Ibid., p. 400.

[5] J. C. B. Soares, "Profiles of a Mandate," Washington, DC: Organization of American States (1994) p. 238.

[6] V. P. Vaky and H. Munoz, *Organization of the American States* (1993) 105.

[7] "Action Plan for the Implementation of the Anti-drug Strategy in the Hemisphere," OAS.CICAD Basic Documents (May 31, 1999), www.cicad.oas.org/en/cicad- basic-documents-strategy-implementation.htm.

[8] Sandy R. Murphy, "Drug Diplomacy and the Supply-Side Strategy: A Survey of United States Practice," *Vanderbilt Law Review* 43 (May 1990), p. 1263.

[9] "The Certification Process," United States State Department (February 1999) www.arc.org.tw/USIA/www. usia.gov/topical/global/drugs/cert98.htm).

[10] Ibid.

[11] Ibid.

[12] "United States Support for Colombia," Fact Sheet released by the Bureau of Western Hemisphere Affairs, United States State Department (March 28, 2000), www.state.gov/www/regions/wha/colombia/fs_000328_americans.html.

[13] "United States Support for Colombia," Fact Sheet released by the Bureau of Western Hemisphere Affairs, United States State Department (28 March, 2000), www.state.gov/www/regions/wha/colombia/fs_000328_plancolombia.html.

[14] David Passage, "Colombia in Turmoil: How the U.S. Could Help," *Special Warfare* (Winter 2000), pp. 12-13.

[15] James Brook, "Brazilian Army Joins War Against Drug Trafficking," *Miami Herald*, International Edition (21 November 1994), p. 3A.

[16] Peter Hakim, "U.S. Drug Certification Process Is in Serious Need of Reform," *Christian Science Monitor* (27 March 1997), p. 15.

[17] Stanley Meiser, "Push to End Certification Intensifies," *Los Angeles Times* (26 March 1997), p. A11.

[18] Robert Novak, "Certifiably Corrupt," *Washington Post* (4 March 1999), p. A21.

[19] Mike Gray, "Texas Heroin Massacre," *Rolling Stone* (27 May 1999), pp. 32-36.

[20] Testimony by DEA agent Richard LaMere before the Senate Caucus on International Narcotics Control, 14 April 1998. Currently, American-made methamphetamine is on the rise, but it is still believed that Mexican "meth" is still predominantly used.

[21] "International Narcotics Control Strategy Report, 1999," Bureau for International Narcotics and Law, United States State Department, March 2000, www.state.gov/www/ global/narcotics_law/1999_narc_report/camex99_part3.html.

[22] George Gedda, "Clinton Says Mexico, Colombia Cooperating in Anti-Drug Efforts" *The Advocate* (2 March 2000), p. 6A.

[23] International Narcotics Control Strategy Report, 1999.

[24] Information provided by the United States Department of Defense Special Operations and Low Intensity Conflict section, under the Office of the Deputy Assistant Secretary of Defense for Drug Enforcement Policy and Support.

[25] Robert Novak, "Certifiably Corrupt."

[26] "US, Mexico, and Drugs," *Christian Science Monitor* (25 September 1998), p. 16.

[27] Scott Park, "Clinton's Mexican Drug Policy is Certifiable Fraud," *Human Events*, 55 (19 March 1999), p. 4.

[28] Ken Dermota, "Snow Business," *World Policy Journal*, 16 (Winter 1999/ 2000), p. 10.

[29] Pomper, "Capital Hosts Annual Ritual."

[30] Ibid.

[31] "Who Should Decertify Whom," *The Wall Street Journal* (4 March 1997), p. A18.

[32] Nick Anderson, "Mexican Drug Certification Faces Attack." *Los Angeles Times Online* (25 March 1999), www.latimes.com:80/excite/990325/ t000026693.html.

[33] Dermota, "Snow Business."

[34] "Colombian President Speaks at U.N., Drugs Found on His Plan," *News Brief Online* (November 1996), accessed 12 January 1999, www.ndsn.org/ NOV96/COLOMBIA.html.

[35] "Restore the Extraditions," *The Miami Herald* (16 April 1997), p. 16A.

[36] Frank Bajak, "Heroin Found on Colombian Leader's Plane," *Washington Post* (22 September 1996), p. A25.

[37] David Lyons, "Smugglers ties Cuba to drugs," *Miami Herald Online*, 10 Oct 1996. 30 Mar 1999 www.fiu.edu/-fcf/smug.castro.html.

[38] "Who Should Decertify Whom," p. A18.

[39] John Thackrah, *Encyclopedia of Terrorism and Political Violence*, p. 165.

[40] Clifford Krauss, "Drug Battle in Bolivia 'Making History': Coca is Cut Back and Could Be Eradicated," *New York Times on the Web* (May 9, 1999),

www.nytimes.com /library/worldamericas/050999bolivia-drugs.html.

[41] Ibid.

CHAPTER 4

[1] A GAP conflict can be likened to the Low Intensity Conflict (LIC) as described earlier.

[2] Max G. Manwaring, *Gray Area Phenomena: Confronting the New World Disorder* Boulder, CO: Westview Press, Inc., (1993), p. xiii.

[3] Manwaring, *Gray Area Phenomena*, p. 65.

[4] Donald J. Mabry, "Andean Drug Trafficking and the Military Option," *Military Review* (March 1990), p. 30.

[5] Definition provided by the Combat Studies Institute, Ft. Leavenworth, KS.

[6] *Field Manual 100-20: Military Operations in Low Intensity Conflict.* Washington, DC: Headquarters, Departments of the Army and Air Force, (1990), 1-1.

[7] Communist organizations won insurgent wars all over the world with this strategy. Communist nations assigned Political Officers to military units, and developed civil indoctrination programs in order to "educate" the people in their ideology, as well as to "inform" them of pertinent current events. The concept was very successful, even though communism as a form of government was not.

[8] *National Drug Control Strategy of 1992.* Washington, DC: The White House, (1992) p. 33.

[9] The "young," or the teenage population, has been the primary target of United States anti-drug policy because young people most easily persuaded to experiment with illegal drugs. They are also, of course, the nation's future hope.

[10] Even though the United States is a primary user of illegal drugs, foreign nations should be included in this education process. Drug use is rising in many foreign countries, particularly in Latin America. There especially education of how narco-terrorism affects their homelands should have a significant impact on reducing foreign drug use.

[11] *National Drug Control Strategy of 1995.* Washington, DC: The White House, (1995), p. 17.

[12] "National Household Survey on Drug Abuse," *Substance Abuse and Mental Health Services Administration* (SAMHSA) (1999).

[13] Tim Friend, "Teen smoking rate highest since 1970s," *USA Today* (24 May 1996), p. 1A

[14] "Graphic Cigarette Warning Labels Don't Impress Teens," *Join Together Online* (5 January 2001), www. jointogether.org/sa/wire/news/ reader.jtml?Object_ID = 265553. Join Together Online credits the Montreal Gazette, 28 December 2000.

[15] Ibid.

[16] D. R. Sparkman, "Risking it All," *Muscle and Fitness* 57.9 (September 1996), p. 124.

[17] Ibid., p. 124.

[18] Ibid., p. 126.

[19] Steve Sternberg, "Survey: Youths Finding Sex, Drugs Too Tempting to Resist," *USA Today* (18 August 1998), p. 11A.

[20] Collett, *The Cocaine Connection*, p. 7.

[21] This author is not implying that Brian Wilson was a drug user, but is only emphasizing the earnestness of the anti-war sentiment during that era.

[22] According to a confidential informant.

[23] This study was conducted 8-9 April 1998 by the author. Assistance was provided by Ph.D. student Heather Honig, and the survey was sponsored by Dr. Brian Bornstein of the Louisiana State University Psychology Department.

[24] Stanton A. Glantz, Patrick Jamieson, "Attitudes Toward Secondhand Smoke, Smoking, and Quitting Among Young People," *Pediatrics*, Vol. 106, No. 6 (December 2000), www.peditrics.org/cgi/content/full/106/6/e82.

[25] "Survey Shows Teens Will Stop Smoking if Harming Others," *Join Together Online* (8 December 2000), www. jointogether.org/sa/wire/news/ reader.jtml?Object_ID = 265314. Join Together Online credits *HealthScout*, 5 December 2000.

[26] Zhou Yongming, *Anti-Drug Crusades in Twentieth-Century China*, New York: Rowman & Littlefield Publishers Inc., (1999), p.3.

[27] Ibid., p. 5.

[28] Manwaring, *Gray Area Phenomena.*

[29] "Peasant Farmers Erupt over Coca Crackdown," *Fayetteville Observer-Times* (25 August 1996), p. 13A.

[30] M. Van Creveld, *Supplying War.* New York: Cambridge University Press (1977), p. 17.

[31] Paul Kennedy, *The Rise and Fall of the Great Powers.* New York: Random House (1987) p. 256.

[32] Alvaro Valencia Tovar, "A View from Bogotá," *Plan Colombia: Some Differing Perspectives.* Implementing Plan Colombia (Special Series), Strategic Studies Institute, U.S. Army War College (June 2001), p.18.

[33] Manwaring, *Gray Area Phenomena*, p. 89.

[34] Ibid., p. 73.

[35] Ibid., p. 90.

[36] Oliver et al., *The International Legal System.*

[37] Blakesley, *Terrorism.*

[38] Ibid., p 103.

[39] Oliver et al., *The International Legal System.*

[40] Blakesley, *Terrorism.*

[41] Ibid., p. 109.

[42] Ibid., p. 125.

[43] Oliver et al., *The International Legal System.*

[44] Blakesley, *Terrorism*, p. 96.

[45] Ibid., p. 117.

[46] Ibid., p. 158.

[47] Ibid.

[48] Ibid.

[49] Ibid., p. 81.

[50] Ibid., p. 58.

[51] Gerardo Bedoya, "Restore the Extraditions," *The Miami Herald* (16 April 1997), p. 16A. (Bedoya was assassinated two days after publishing these words.)

[52] W. R. LaFave and A. W. Scott Jr., *Criminal Law. Hornbook Series Student Edition*, 2nd ed., St. Paul, MN: West Publishing Co., (1986), p. 617.

[53] Blakesley, *Terrorism*, p. 120.

[54] Most likely, drug addicts would not be good candidates for the extradition theory. During China's successful fight against opium in the communist era addiction was treated as a sickness, not a crime. Addiction occurs when someone no longer has the self-control to make their own decision about their habit, regardless of the penalty.

[55] 60% of the students surveyed claimed not to be drug users at the time of the study.

[56] Author's interview with confidential source, Baton Rouge, Louisiana, February, 1998.

[57] Antiterrorism and Effective Death Penalty Act of 1996, Pub. L No. 104-132. Sec. 303, *Prohibition on Terrorist Fundraising.*

[58] No legislation currently exists to extradite United States citizens. Therefore, circumstances would need to be covered under a specific treaty.

[59] Blakesley, *Terrorism*, p. 311.

[60] Andres Talero, "Colombian Government Better Served by Truth than by Scapegoats," Letter, *The Miami Herald. International Edition* (2 May 1995), p. A12. (Talero is a Colombian businessman and former Consul General in Miami.)

[61] Reprinted in C. T. Oliver et al., *The International Legal System*, p. 1386.

[62] Some countries put greater emphasis on using the National Guard. The United States uses it to some extent, while Venezuela uses it much more.

[63] G. H. Williams and S. C. Williams, "America's Drug Policy: Who Are the Addicts?" *Iowa Law Review* 75 (May 1990), pp. 1119-1133.

[64] Sandy R. Murphy, "Drug Diplomacy and the Supply-Side Strategy: A Survey of United States Practice," *Vanderbilt Law Review* 43 (May 1990), pp.

1260-1309.

[65]Ibid.

[66] K. Ellison, "Argentina's New Role in the Drug War," *The Miami Herald* (1 May 1997), p. 18A.

[67] Manwaring, *Gray Area Phenomena*, 130.

[68] Taken from remarks by OAS Secretary General Dr. Cesar Gavira at the Inter-American Specialized Conference on Terrorism, Lima, Peru, 26 April 1996.

[69] J. N. Moore, G. B. Roberts, and R. F. Turner, *National Security Law* (Durham, NC: Carolina Academic Press, 1990), p. xxxv.

[70] L. E. Nagle, "The Rule of Law or the Rule of Fear: Some Thoughts on Colombian Extradition," *Loyola of Los Angeles International and Comparative Law Journal* 13 (1991), p. 863.

[71] S. A. Gardner, "A Global Initiative to Deter Drug Trafficking: Will Internationalizing the Drug War Work?" *Temple International and Comparative Law Journal* 7 (Fall 1993): 305.

[72] S. Dycus, A. L. Berney, W. C. Banks, and P. Raven-Hansen, *National Security Law*, 2nd ed. (Boston: Little, Brown and Company, 1997), p. 333.

[73] It was not known at the time that one of the Barbary States, Tripoli, had declared war on the United States.

[74] The Posse Comitatus Act was enacted just after the American Civil War as a result of interference by the Union army in civil affairs of former Confederate States.

[75] Congress did enact an exception to the act which authorizes the military to provide indirect support and select training to law enforcement, and to provide or operate select military equipment to assist in drug enforcement, immigration, and tariffs.

[76] In Moore, Tipson, and Turner's ranking of the nine most dangerous threats to a nation, they put subversion and intimidation as number four and five, respectively (*National Security Law*, p. 17).

[77] Moore et al., *National Security Law*, p. 17.

[78] J. N. Moore et al., *National Security Law Documents*. Durham, NC: Carolina Academic Press, (1995). (As per the Definition of Aggression Resolution.)

[79] C. T. Oliver, E. B. Firmage, C. L. Blakesley, R. F. Scoot, and S. A. Williams, *Documentary Supplement to Cases and Materials on the International Legal System*, 4th ed., Westbury, NY: The Foundation Press, Inc., (1995) pp. 278-279.

[80] Gardner, "Will Internationalizing the Drug War Work?" p. 290. (In 1987 the Medellin Cartel was recognized as a "power unto itself" when it was estimated to have revenues of $8 billion U.S. dollars).

[81] Murphy, "Drug Diplomacy."

[82] J. Dizon, "Getting Serious About Winning America's Drug War," *American Journal of Criminal Law* 24 (Spring 1997), pp. 463-469.

[83] The words "now believe" were used to state the question after reading the main text.

[84] Interestingly, several students changed their answer to "no" after reading the text. One student stated he feared the U.S. military could not take on the powerful narco-supported terrorist-insurgent organizations. Another claimed to have a friend in the U.S. military, and did not want to see him sent off to fight such a powerful enemy.

[85] Moore et al., *National Security Law*, p. 172.

[86] Rother, "U.S. Official Proposes $1 Billion for Colombian Drug War."

[87] Larry Rother, "Colombia Is Reeling, Hurt by Rebels and Economy," *New York Times* (18 July 1999), p. 3.

[88] Moore et al., *National Security Law*, p. 86.

[89] The Mansfield Agreement of 1976 was established in response to the torture of an individual arrested for extradition to the United States, in which U.S. agents were allegedly involved.

[90] C. A. Donesa, "Protecting National Interests: The Legal Status of Extraterritorial Law Enforcement by the Military," *Duke Law Journal* 41 (February 1992), p. 873.

[91] Ibid., p. 874.

[92] Donesa, Ibid, and Williams, "America's Drug Policy."

[93] Some critics view such threats as Panama in 1989 and Haiti in 1994 as lesser threats to security than the drug war. Dizon, for example, in "Getting

Serious About Winning America's Drug War," provides a pertinent analysis of V.T. Bugliosi's book *The Phoenix Project.*

[94] Dycus et al., *National Security Law*, p. 374.

[95] Oliver et al., *Documentary Supplement*, p. 1295.

[96] Noriega was asked by the U.S. government to step down, but of course he refused.

[97] Oliver et al., *Documentary Supplement*, p. 1300.

[98] Murphy, "Drug Diplomacy," p. 1281.

[99] Ibid., In the United States, the military is limited to surveillance (in special cases) and support activities.

[100] H. Grotius, *On the Law of War and Peace*, trans. F. W. Kelsey, Oxford, England: Oxford University Press, (1925) p. 628. (Original work published 1646).

[101] Murphy, "Drug Diplomacy," p. 1288.

[102] Some believe that the Laws of Proportionality were exceeded by the United States during the Panama invasion. Others believe that international law should not use the laws of proportionality in second-guessing the tactical judgements of what military forces are required to achieve an objective (Oliver et al., *The International Legal System*, p. 1294). Perhaps the denial of armor by the Clinton administration to support a key military operation in Somalia, which ended in failure, is a prime example of this.

[103] A. P. V. Rogers, *Law on the Battlefield.* Manchester, UK: Manchester University Press, (1996), p. 16. (From the Department of Defense Report, 116.)

[104] U.S. Army Special Forces Command, Fort Bragg, NC (1995).

[105] Murphy, "Drug Diplomacy."

[106] One could ask if U.S. forces are required at all. It should be noted here that U.S. equipment sold outright to foreign states for counter-narcotics operations is often used against neighbors with whom they have a squabble. If the United States is going to provide the majority of the funds for this force (as it probably will), a U.S. government presence is desired to ensure U.S. funds are being used as desired.

[107] Williams, G. H., and Williams, S. C. "America's Drug Policy: Who Are the Addicts?" *Iowa Law Review* 75 (May 1990), p. 1125.

[108] Authored by foreign officers attending the U.S. Army Command and General Staff course at Ft. Leavenworth. Authors: COL Cureau, Brazil; LTC Pereia, Honduras; LTC Ruggeri, Italy; LTC Castellanos, Mexico; LTC Thonglek, Thailand; LTC Cedeno, Venezuela; LTC Miranda, Venezuela; MAJ Lamas, Argentina.

[109] Cureau et al., *Drug Control Strategy*, p. 4.

[110] Ibid., p. 36.

[111] There is a legitimate fear that a combined Latin American force would allow the United States and larger Latin American powers to impose their wills on the domestic affairs of weaker states (Vaky and Munoz, *Organization of the American States*, p. 44). Measures must be implemented to prevent this.

[112] Manwaring, *Gray Area Phenomena*.

[113] Donesa, "Protecting National Interests."

[114] W. M. Gianaris, "The New World Order and the Need for an International Court," *Fordham International Law Journal* 16, (1992-1993). Pp. 88-119.

[115] Moore et al., *National Security Law*, p. 175.

[116] Ibid., p. 175.

[117] An effort to put the drug war under the exclusive domain of the United Nations was offered under the justification that the drug problem is a "threat to international peace and security," but seven of the ten nonpermanent members of the Security Council blocked the effort for the above stated reason (Williams and Williams, *America's Drug Policy*.

[118] Moore et al., *National Security Law*, p. 175.

[119] Walter. G. Sharp, Sr., "Protecting the Avatars of International Peace and Security," *Duke Journal of Contemporary and International Law* 7 (Fall 1996), p. 109.

[120] Ibid., p. 138.

[121] Ibid., 139.

[122] Christopher Greenwood, "Protection of Peacekeepers: The Legal Regime," *Duke Journal of Contemporary and International Law* 7(Fall 1996), pp. 185-207.

[123] A military term used to describe the required conditions that, when achieved, attain the strategic objective.

[124] Pedro Arenas, "A 'Paradise Lost' In the Colombian Amazon," *Christian Science Monitor* (2 December 1997), p. 19.

[125] "Brazil: Drug Cartels Using Amazon's Natives," *The Dominion Post* (30 May 99), p. 2-A.

[126] Due to the poor soil conditions in parts of South America (such as the Upper Huallaga Valley in Peru), the durable coca has been one of the few plants capable of thriving. The plant was originally used by religious leaders among the Incas for its mystical euphoric results. The Spanish Conquistadors expanded its cultivation when they discovered that the Native American slaves who worked in the silver and gold mines were able to handle larger workloads under its influence. (The plant was found to reduce hunger, fatigue and boredom). In the late 1970s, when cocaine use began to soar, large numbers of farmers turned to growing coca to supplement their otherwise meager wages. A peasant could be make over three times as much money for growing coca (Tarazona-Sevillano, *Sendero Luminoso*). Additionally, coca is an easy plant to grow, requiring little attention, while cultivating a plant such as hemp (marijuana) is highly intensive (Collett, *The Cocaine Connection*).

[127] Jeffry J. Schott, *Prospects for Free Trade in the Americas*, Institute for International Economics, Washington, DC (2001), p. 33-38.

[128] Ibid., p. 33.

[129] Joseph R. Nunez, "Fighting the Hobbesian Trinity in Colombia: A New Strategy for Peace," Strategic Studies Institute, U.S. Army War College, April 2001. Nunez credits Frances Stewart and Albert Berry, "Liberalization and Inequality," in *Inequality, Globalization and World Politics*, Andrew Hurrel and Ngaire Woods, eds., Oxford: Oxford University Press (1999), p. 172.

[130] Albert Coll, "United States Strategic Interests in Latin America," *Journal of Interamerican Studies and World Affairs* (Spring 1997), p. 53. Coll credits *The Economist*, "The Backlash in Latin America 30 November-6 December 1996), p. 19.

[131] Harry Patrinos, "The Cost of Discrimination," *Studies in Comparative International Development*, 35, No. 2,(Summer 2000).

[132] Larry Rother, "Drugs! Aliens! Washington, Wake Up," *New York Times* (4 May 1997), p. E3.

[133] "Lagging Reforms," *The Economist* (30 November 1996), reprinted in *World Press Review* (March 1997), p. 7.

[134] Gary Wynia, *The Politics of Latin American Development*, 3rd ed., New York: Cambridge University Press, (1990) p. 125.

[135] Ibid., p. 115.

[136] Paul Kennedy, *The Rise and Fall of the Great Powers*, p. 446.

[137] Remarks by President G.W. Bush in announcement of the director of the office of drug control policy, 10 May 2001.

[138] Cureau et al., *Drug Control Strategy*.

[139] Schott, *Prospects for Free Trade*, p. 2.

[140] It must be noted that NAFTA has not yet ended Mexico's problems of corruption, but it could also be said that the lucrative drug trade is allowing corruption to continue.

[141] Schott, *Prospects for Free Trade*, pp. 91-92.

[142] Ibid., p. 109.

CHAPTER 5

[1] While this strategy would stop the use of drugs from international sources, there is a good chance it could cause drugs domestically produced to remain the same, or even increase, which is why current anti-drug education efforts are still important. However, as this strategy eliminates drugs from entering the country from outside our borders, it allows our counterdrug law enforcement agencies to now focus on a "one front war"—the domestic arena. This would greatly enhance our efforts in fighting the domestically produced illegal drug problem.

[2] R. H. Bailey, *Battles for Atlanta* Alexandria, VA: Time-Life Books (1985) p. 20.

[3] Released by the Bureau for International Narcotics and Law Enforcement Affairs, U.S. State Department. Washington, D.C., March 1998.

[4] The Financial Action Task Force goes after the illegal financial profits of the drug lords, and has been remarkably effective (Manwaring, *Gray Area Phenomena*).

[5] F. Wilkenson, "A Separate Peace," *Rolling Stone* (May 5, 1994), p. 28.

[6] Dycus et al., *National Security Law*, p. 601.

Bibliography

"Action Plan for the Implementation of the Anti-drug Strategy in the Hemisphere." OAS.CICAD Basic Documents. (31 May 1999), http://www.cicad.oas.org/en/cicad-basic-documents-strategy-implementation.html.

Adams, James. *The Financing of Terror.* New York: Simon and Schuster, 1986.

"American Drug Aid Goes South." *New York Times* (25 November 1996), p. A14.

Anderson, Nick. "Mexican Drug Certification Faces Attack." *Los Angeles Times* (25 March 1999), http://www.latimes.com:80/excite/990325/t000026693.html.

"Antiterrorism and Effective Death Penalty Act of 1996." Pub. L No. 104-132. Sec 303, Prohibition of Terrorist Fundraising.

Arenas, Pedro. "A 'Paradise Lost' in the Colombian Amazon." *Christian Science Monitor* (2 December 1997), p. 19.

Arostegui, Martin. "Castro's Scapegoat." *National Review* 25 (28 November 1992), pp. 33-35.

Arostegui, Martin. "Return of the Godfather, Part II." *National Review* 12 (30 January 1997). pp. 25-26.

Bailey, R. H. *Battles for Atlanta.* Alexandria, VA: Time-Life Books, 1985.

Bajak, Frank. "Heroin Found on Colombian leader's plane." *Washington Post* (22 September 1996), p. A25.

Barraclough, Colin. "Iran Confronts a Long-Hidden Problem: Drugs," *New York Times Online* (29 August 1999), www.nytimes.com/library/world/mideast/082999iran-drugs.html.

Bedoya, Gerardo. "Restore the Extraditions." *Miami Herald* (16 April 1997), p. 16A.

Beres, Louis R. "The Legal Meaning of Terrorism for the Military Commander." *Connecticut Journal of International Law* 11 (May 1995), pp. 2-27.

Black's Law Dictionary. 4th ed. St. Paul, MN: West Publishing Co, 1951.

Blakesley, C. L. *Terrorism, Drugs, International Law, and the Protection of Human Liberty.* Ardsley, NY: Transnational Publishers, 1992.

Bonner, R. "A Reporter at Large: Peru's War." <u>New Yorker</u> (4 January 1988), pp. 31-58

Booth, Martin. *Opium: A History.* New York: St. Martin's Press, 1996.

Booth, Martin. *The Dragon Syndicates.* New York: Carroll & Graf Publishers, 1999.

"Brazil Drug Cartels Using Amazon's Natives." *The Dominion Post* (30 May 1999), p. 2-A.

Brodzinsky, Sibylla. "Guerrillas Threaten Colombia's Peace Effort." *USA Today* (8 December 1999), p. 24A.

Brook, James. "Brazilian Army Joins War Against Drug Trafficking." *Miami Herald,* International Edition (21 November 1994), p. 3A.

Brooks, Laura. "Colombian Insurgents Threaten Elections." *Washington Times* (14 October 1997): A13.

Campbell, A. B. "The *Ker-Frisbie* Doctrine: A Jurisdictional Weapon in the War on Drugs." *Vanderbilt Journal of Transnational Law* 13 (1990), pp. 385-434.

Chang, Iris. *The Rape of Nanking.* New York:

Basic Books, 1997.

Clutterbuck, Richard. *Terrorism and Guerrilla Warfare.* New York: Routledge, 1990.

Coll, Albert. "United States Strategic Interests in Latin America. An Assessment." *Journal of Inter-American Studies and World Affairs* 39 (Spring 1997), pp. 45-57.

Collett, Merrill. *The Cocaine Connection.* Ephrata, PA: Science Press, 1989.

Collett, Merrill. "The Myth of the Narco-Guerrillas." *The Nation* (13 August 1988).

"Colombia Advance of the Russian Mafia." (Excerpts by Alirio Fernando Bustos, *El Tiempo) Reserve Officer Association National Security Report* (July 1999), p. 38.

"Colombia Calls for Arms from Uncle Sam." The Economist (25 September–1 October 1999), p. 38.

"Colombia in the Long Shadow of War" *The Economist* (17-23 July 1999), pp. 31-32.

"Colombian Authorities Link Guerrillas to Drug-Traffickers." *Special Warfare* (Winter 1997), p. 37.

"Colombian Dreams of Peace." *The Economist* (15-21 May 1999), pp. 37-38.

"Colombian President Speaks at U.N., Drugs Found on His Plane." *News Brief Online*, (November 1996), www.ndsn. org/NOV96/COLOMBIA. html).

"Colombian Rebels Kidnap 100 at Mass but Later Let Most Go." *New York Times* (31 May 1999), http://nytimes.com/

yr/mo/day/news/world/colombia-kidnapping.html.

"Colombian Rebels Kill 24." *Fayetteville Observer-Times* (21 September 1995), p. 16A.

Crossette, Barbara. "War on Drugs Urged at U.N. by Colombia." *New York Times* (24 September 1996), p. A1.

Crozier, Brian. "The Castro Connection." *National Review* 4 (5 March 1990), p. 31.

Cureau, Pereia, Ruggeri, Castellanos, Thonglek, Cedeno, Miranda, and Lamas. "US National Drug Control Strategy: Impact on LATAM," 1990. Unpublished manuscript, US Army Command and General Staff College at Fort Leavenworth, KS.

Darling, Juanita. "Newest Cocaine Route to States: The Caribbean." *Los Angeles Times* (27 April 1997), p. A12.

Department of Defense definition of narco-terrorism online (12 January 1999), www.mil/doctrine/jel/doddoct/ data/n/04033/htm.

Dermota, Ken. "Snow Business." *World Policy Journal* 16 (Winter 1999/2000), p. 10.

"The Disputatious Diplomacy of Drugs." *The Economist* (11-17 September 1999), pp. 37-38.

Dizon, Jason. "Getting Serious About Winning America's Drug War." *American Journal of Criminal Law* 24 (Spring 1997), pp. 463-469.

Donesa, Christopher A. "Protecting National Interests: The Legal Status of Extraterritorial Law Enforcement by the Military." *Duke Law Journal* 41 (February 1992), pp. 867-906.

"Drug Trafficking May Fund North Korean Regime." *Special Warfare*, 7, 4 (October 1994), pp. 52-53.

Duncan, Raymond. *The Soviet Union and Cuba: Interests and Influences.* New York: Praeger, 1985.

Dycus, S., Berney, A. L., Banks, W. C., and Raven-Hansen, P. *National Security Law*, 2nd ed. Boston: Little, Brown and Company, 1997.

Dziedzic, Michael J. "The Organization of American States and Drug Control." In MacDonald, S. B., & Zagaris, B., Eds., *International Handbook on Drug Control.* Westport, CT: Greenwood Press (1992), pp. 397-414.

Ehrenfeld, Rachel. *Narco-terrorism.* New York: Basic Books, 1990.

Ellison, K. "Argentina's New Role in the Drug War." *Miami Herald* (1 May 1997), p. 18A.

"Exile Files Drug Complaint Against Castro." *Miami Herald* (7 January 1999), www.nocastro.com/voicesexildrug. html).

Farah, Douglas. "Caribbean Key to U.S. Drug Trade." *Washington Post* (23 September 1996), p. A1.

Farah, Douglas. "Russian Mob, Drug Cartels Joining Forces." *Washington Post* (29 September 1997), p. A1.

Farah, Douglas. "New Threat From Colombia: Heroin." *The Washington Post* (27 March 1997), p. A1.

"The Ferghana Valley," *Jane's for Intelink*, 28 August 2001, janes.ic.gov/cgi-bin/texis/bin/se...x_eUqO -?this_edition+jir2001&itemnum=30.

Fernández, Alina, *Castro's Daughter: An Exile's Memoir of Cuba.* NY: St. Martin's Griffin, 1999.

Field Manual (Army) 100-5: Operations. Washington DC: Headquarters, Department of the Army, 1993.

Field Manual (Army) 100-20: Military Operations in Low Intensity Conflict. Washington DC: Headquarters, Department of the Army and Air Force, 1990.

Fitz-simons, D. W. "Sendero Luminoso: Case Study in Insurgency." *Parameters* XXIII, 2 (1993), p. 69.

Franck, T. M. & Glennon, M. J. *Foreign Relations and National Security Law*, 2nd ed., St. Paul, MN: West Publishing Co., 1993.

Friend, Tim. "Teen Smoking Rate Highest Since 1970s." *USA Today* (24 May 1996), p. 1A.

Gahlinger, Paul. Interview. "Could the war on terror help reduce the world's supply of illegal narcotics?" Fox and Friends, FoxNews, 19 November 2001.

Garcia, Guillermo. "FBI Scours Mexico Grave Site." *USA Today* (1 December 1999), p. 1A.

Gardner, S. A. "A Global Initiative to Deter Drug Trafficking: Will Internationalizing the Drug War Work?" *Temple International and Comparative Law Journal* 7 (Fall 1993), pp. 287-317.

Gertz, Bill. "Bin Laden Terror Group Tries to Acquire Chemical Arms." *Washington Times* (26 September 2001), p. A3.

Glantz, Stanton A. and Jamieson, Patrick. "Attitudes Toward Secondhand Smoke, Smoking, and Quitting Among Young People." Pediatrics, Vol 106, No. 6 (December 2000), www.peditrics.org/cgi/content/full/106/6/e82.

Gianaris, William M. "The New World Order and the Need for an International Court." *Fordham International Law Journal* 16 (1992-1993), pp. 88-119.

Greenwood, Christopher. "Protection of Peacekeepers: The Legal Regime." *Duke Journal of Contemporary and International Law* 7 (Fall 1996), pp. 185-207.

Gorriti, Gustavo. "Peru's Prophet of Terror." *Reader's Digest* (September 1992), pp. 93-98.

Gray, Mike. "Texas Heroin Massacre." *Rolling Stone* (27 May 1999), pp. 32-36.

Grotius, Hugo. *On the Law of War and Peace.* F. W. Kelsey, trans. Oxford, England: Oxford University Press, 1925. (Original work published 1646).

Gugliotta, G., & Leen, J. *Kings of Cocaine.* New York: Harper Paperbacks, 1990.

Hakim, Peter. "U.S. Drug Certification Process is in Serious Need of Reform." *Christian Science Monitor* (27 March 1997), p. 15.

Hargrove, Thomas. R. *Long March to Freedom.* NY: Ballantine Books, 1995.

"Indian Security Challenged by Narcoterrorists." *Special Warfare* (October 1994), p. 52.

Johnson, T. "Colombians Fear Rebel 'Peace Zone.'" *Miami Herald* (10 August 1998), pp. A1, 12A.

Johnson, T. "Rebels Wipe Out Anti-Narcotics Base." *Miami Herald* (6 August 1998), pp. A1, 16A.

Join Together Online, www.jointogether.org.

Kennedy, Paul. *The Rise and Fall of the Great Powers.* New York: Random House, 1987.

Kolton, Randy (Major, U.S. Army). "Combating the Colombian Drug Cartels." *Military Review* (March 1990), pp. 49-63.

Krauss, Clifford. "Drug Battle in Bolivia 'Making History:' Coca is Cut Back and Could Be Eradicated." *New York Times* (9 May 1999), www.nytimes.com/library/World/ americas/050999bolivia-drugs.html).

LaFave, W. R., and Scott, A. W. Jr. *Criminal Law.* Hornbook series student edition, 2nd ed., St. Paul, MN: West Publishing Co., 1986.

LaFranchi, H. "Colombia Calls Its Rebel Armies the 'New Cartels.'" *Christian Science Monitor* (21 October 1996), p. 6.

"Lagging Reforms." *The Economist* (30 November 1996), reprinted in *World Press Review* (March 1997), p. 7.

Laqueur, Walter. "Reflections on Terrorism," *Foreign Affairs,* 65, 1986, pp. 86-88; reprinted in C. T. Oliver, E. B. Firmage, C. L. Blakesley, R. F. Scott, and S. A. Williams, eds., *The International Legal System,* Westbury, NY: The Foundation Press, Inc., 1995.

"Latin America Overview." U.S. State Department (27 February 1999) http://state.gov.www/global///terrorism/1997

Report/latin.html).

Lintner, Bertil. *Cross-border drug trade in the Golden Triangle (S.E. Asia).* Durham, UK: Boundaries Research Press, 1991.

Lyons, David. "Smuggler's Ties Cuba to Drugs." *Miami Herald* (10 October 1996), www.fiu.edu/fcf/smug.Castro. html.

Mabry, Donald. "Andean Drug Trafficking and the Military Option." *Military Review* (March 1990), pp. 29-40.

Manwaring, Max G. *Gray Area Phenomena.* Boulder, CO: Westview Press, Inc, 1993.

Manwaring, Max G. "U.S. Security Policy in the Western Hemisphere." *Implementing Plan Colombia* (Special Series) Strategic Studies Institute, U.S. Army War College (June 2001), p. 11.

McIntyre, Jamie. "U.S. Considering Targeting Taliban Drug Trade," *CNN.com* (24 September 2001), www.cnn.com/ 2001/US/09/24/ret.taliban.drugs/.

Meiser, Stanley. "Push to End Certification Intensifies." *Los Angeles Times* (26 March 1997), p. A11.

"Messages of War." *The Economist* (29 May–4 June 1999), p. 37.

Meyer, Dan C. "The Myth of Narcoterrorism in Latin America." *Military Review* (March 1990), pp. 64-70.

Moore, J. N., Tipson F. S., and Turner, R. F. *National Security Law.* Durham, NC: Carolina Academic Press, 1990.

Moore, J. N., Roberts, G. B., and Turner, R. F. *National Security Law Documents.* Durham, NC: Carolina Academic Press, 1995.

Morrison, James. "Targeting of Narco-Rebels." *Washington Times* (15 July 1997), p. 12.

Mufson, Steve, "Updated List designates 28 Groups as Terrorist." *Washington Post* (6 October 2001), p. A20.

Mullem, Francis Jr. "Cuban Government Involvement in Drug Trafficking." Testimony before the House Committee Foreign Affairs, Task Force on International Narcotics Control (21 February 1984).

Murphy, Sandy R. "Drug Diplomacy and the Supply-Side Strategy: A Survey of United States Practice." *Vanderbilt Law Review* 43 (May 1990), pp. 1260-1309.

Nagle, Luz E. "The Rule of Law or the Rule of Fear: Some Thoughts on Colombian Extradition." *Loyola of Los Angeles International and Comparative Law Journal* 13 (1991), pp. 851-870.

"Narcotics: Terror's Ally." *US News and World Report* (4 May 1987), pp. 30-37.

Navarro, Mireya. "Russian Submarine Drifts Into Center of Brazen Drug Plot." *New York Times* (7 March 1997), p. A22.

Novak, Robert. "Certifiably Corrupt." *Washington Post* (4 March 1999), p. A21.

Nunez, Joseph R. "Fighting the Hobbesian Trinity in Colombia: A New Strategy for Peace." Strategic Studies Institute, U.S. Army War College, April 2001.

Oliver, C. T., Firmage, E. B., Blakesley, C. L., Scoot, R. F., and Williams, S. A. *The International Legal System.* Westbury, NY: The Foundation Press, Inc., 1995.

Oliver, C. T., Firmage, E. B., Blakesley, C. L., Scoot, R. F., and Williams, S. A. *Documentary Supplement to Cases and Materials on the International Legal System*, 4th ed., Westbury, NY: The Foundation Press, Inc., 1995.

Oppenheimer, Andres. *Bordering on Chaos.* Boston: Little, Brown and Company, 1996.

"Pakistan Sponsored Narco-terrorism in India." Papers from the *Indian Defense Review* (12 January 1999),

www.geocities.com/The Tropics/3328/idr00007/html.

Palmer, David. "Peru, The Drug Business and the Shining Path." *Journal of Inter-American Studies and World Affairs* 3, 34 (Fall 1992), pp. 65-87.

Park, Scott. "Clinton's Mexican Drug Policy is Certifiable Fraud." *Human Events* 55 (19 March 1999),p. 4.

Patrinos, Harry. "The Cost of Discrimination," *Studies in Comparative International Development*, 35, 2 (Summer 2000).

"Peace in Colombia? This Year, Next year, Sometime." *The Economist* (10-16 April 1999), p. 31.

"Peasant Farmers Erupt Over Coca Crackdown." *Fayetteville Observer-Times* (25 August 1996), p. 13A.

"Peru's Drug Successes Erodes as Traffickers Adapt." *New York Times* (19 August 1999), www.nytimes.com/library/ world/americas/081999peru-drugs.htm.

"Peru's Sendero Luminoso Still Has Teeth." *Special Warfare* (Winter 1999), p. 47.

Proenza, Anne. "Mother of Courage." Le Monde, Paris. (5-6 January 1997). As published in *World Press Review* (March 1997), p. 9.

Pomper, Miles, and Gowda, Vanita. "Capitol Hill Hosts Annual Ritual: Alternately Warning and Encouraging Mexico on Anti-Drug Campaigns." *CQ Weekly* 57 (2 February 1999), p. 501.

"Puerto Rico: A Favorite Of Cartels." *Washington Post* (16 February 1998), p. A22.

"Rancher Tells of Drug Gangs Intimidation." *Fayetteville Observer-Times* (1 August 1996), p. 3A.

"Report: Arms Dealers Feeding Burundi War." *USA Today* (10 August 1995), p. 8A.

"Restore the Extraditions." *Miami Herald* (16 April 1997), p. 16A.

Reuter, P. and Ronfeldt, D. "Quest for Integrity: The Mexican-U.S. Drug Issue in the 1980s." *Journal of Inter-American Studies and World Affairs* 34 (Fall 1992), pp. 89-153.

"A Revolution Peru's Rebels Didn't Intend." *New York Times* (29 August 1999),www.nytimes.com/library/world/americas/082999perurevolution.html.

Richey, Warren. "Miami Vice II: The Smugglers Return." *Christian Science Monitor* (2 January 1998), p. 1.

Rogers, A. P. V. *Law on the Battlefield.* Manchester, UK: Manchester University Press, 1996.

Ross, Brian. "The Cuban Connection." NBC Nightly News (29 September 1982).

Rother, Larry. "Colombia is Reeling, Hurt by Rebels and Economy." *New York Times* (18 July 1999), p. 3.

Rother, Larry. "Drugs! Aliens! Washington, Wake Up." *New York Times* (4 May 1997), p. E3.

Rother, Larry. "Fishing for Ransom, Colombian Rebels Cast Net Wide." *New York Times* (3 June 1999), www.nytimes. com/library/world/americas/060399colombia-kidnapping.htm.

Rother, Larry. "Haiti Paralysis Brings a Boom in Drug Trade." *New York Times* (27 October 1998), p. A1.

Rother, Larry, and Wren, Christopher. "U.S. Official Proposes $1 Billion for Colombian Drug War." *New York Times* (17 July 1999), p. A5.

Rouke, John T. *International Politics and the World Stage.* 5th ed. Guilford, CT: Brown and Benchmark Publishers, 1995.

Scarborough, Rowan. "Global Command Considered." *Washington Times online,* 23 October 2001.

Schott, Jeffry J. *Prospects for Free Trade in the Americas.* Institute for International Economics, Washington DC, 2001.

"Sedative Being Smuggled Into U.S." *Fayetteville Observer-Times* (2 April 1995), p. 16A.

Seper, Jerry. "Taliban Threatens to Add Opium to Arsenal," *Washington Times* (27 September 2001), p. 14.

Sharp, Walter G. Sr. "Protecting the Avatars of International Peace and Security." *Duke Journal of Contemporary and International Law* 7 (Fall 1996), pp. 93-183.

Shifter, Michael. "Colombia on the Brink." *Foreign Affairs* (Jul/Aug 1999), pp. 14-20.

Soares, J. C. B. *Profiles of a Mandate.* Organization of American States, 1994.

Sparkman, Dennis R. "Risking It All." *Muscle and Fitness,* 57, 9 (September 1996), pp. 123-126.

Sternberg, Steve. "Survey: Youths Finding Sex, Drugs Too Tempting to Resist." *USA Today* (14 August 1998), p. 11A.

Substance Abuse and Mental Health Services Administration (SAMHSA). "National Household Survey on Drug Abuse." 1999.

Sun Tzu. "The Art of War." Trans. Giles, Lionel. In *Roots of Strategy*, ed. Phillips, T. R. Harrisburg, PA: Stackpole, 1985.

Talero, Andres. "Colombian Government Better Served by Truth Than by Scapegoats" [Letter to the Editor]. *Miami Herald*, International Edition (2 May 1995), p. A12.

Tarazona-Sevellano, G., and Rueter, J. B. *Sendero Luminoso and the Threat of Narco-terrorism*. New York: Praeger Publishers, 1990.

Taylor, Carl S. "Gang Imperialism." In *Gangs in America*, ed. C. Ronald Huff. Newbury Park, CA: Sage Publications, Inc., (1990), pp. 103-115.

"Terrorismo Dejo Hasta Hoy 131,700 Ninos en Orfandad" [Terrorism Leaves 131,700 Children Orphans to Date]. *La Republica* (27 October 1995), p. 10.

Thackrah, John. *Encyclopedia of Terrorism and Political Violence*. New York: Routledge and Kegan Paul Inc., 1987.

"Tot Slain in Wrong Turn Onto 'Avenue of Killers.'" *USA Today* (19 September 1995), p. 3A.

"Transnational Crime and Terrorism." *Jane's for Intelink*, 1 August 2001, janes.ic.gov/cgi-bin/texis/bin/se...x_eUqO-?this_edition+jir2001& itemnum=24.

U.S. Department of Defense Directive 0-2000.12-H (February 1993).

U.S. Department of State. "The Certification Process." (February 1999), www.arc.org.tw/USIA/www.usia.gov/ tropical/global/drugs/cert98.html.

U.S. Department of State. International Narcotics Control Strategy Report, 1999. Released by the Bureau for International Narcotics and Law Enforcement Affairs, Washington, DC, March 2000.

U.S. Government Accounting Office (US-GAO). "The Drug War: U.S. Programs in Peru Face Serious Obstacles" (Report to Congressional requesters; GAO/NS/AD 92-36). Washington D.C.: US-GAO, October 1991.

U.S. Senate, Republican Policy Committee. The Kosovo Liberation Army: Does the Clinton Policy Support Group with Terror, Drug Ties?" March 31, 1999.

"US, Mexico, and Drugs." *Christian Science Monitor* (25 September 1998):, p. 16.

Vaky, V. P., & Munoz, H. *The Future of the Organization of the American States.* New York: The Twentieth Century Fund Press, 1993.

Van Creveld, Martin. *Supplying War.* New York: Cambridge University Press, 1977.

Valencia Tovar, Alvaro. "A View from Bogotá." In *Plan Colombia: Some Differing Perspectives.* Implementing Plan Colombia (Special Series). Strategic Studies Institute, U.S. Army War College (June 2001), p.18.

"Warpaths." *The Economist* (24-30 July 1999), p. 34.

Weible, J. "Missing Russian Nukes, New Movie Raises Furor." *Army Times* (20 October 1997), p. 45.

Weymouth, Lally. "Battling 'the Bad Guys,'" *Newsweek* (14 Feb 2000), p. 50.

White House, The. *National Drug Control Strategy.* Washington DC: The White House (1992, 1995, & 1998).

"Who Should Decertify Whom." *Wall Street Journal* (4 March 1997), p. A18.

Wilkenson, F. "A Separate Peace." *Rolling Stone,* 681 (5 May 1994), pp. 26-28.

Williams, G. H., and Williams, S. C. "America's Drug Policy: Who Are the Addicts?" *Iowa Law Review* 75 (May 1990), pp. 1119-1133.

Williams, Phil. "Drugs and Guns." *Bulletin of the Atomic Scientists* 55 (January/February 1999), p. 46.

Wilson, G. "The Changing Game: The United States Evolving Supply-Side Approach to Narcotics Trafficking." *Vanderbilt Journal of Transnational Law* (26 January 1994), pp. 1163-1209.

Wynia, Gary W. *The Politics of Latin American Development,* 3rd ed. NY: Cambridge University Press, 1990.

Yongming, Zhou. *Anti-Drug Crusades in Twentieth-Century China.* New York: Rowman & Littlefield Publishers, Inc., 1999.

Index